Can I Be Real?

A way to become comfortable having
uncomfortable conversations about race.

By: Marc Hardy

I would like to dedicate this book to Lizzy. You've had my back ever since the day I met you in Chemistry class over ten years ago. You're a blessing. To my mom, who would give us her last heartbeat, I thank you. Lastly, to my best friends Wes, Jamel, Q, DJ, Darius and Cordaryl, you all keep me inspired more than you know.

<u>Disclaimer</u>

I'm a first time author whose only goal is to get people to empower themselves. You don't have to hold some high government office or have a million followers to create solutions to some of our nation's most prominent issues. To do this, I need people to understand that these issues actually do exist and they are plaguing our communities. I do not claim to be an expert in any of the following content but I hope that I can get you to seek out ways to do your part in leaving a better country for our future generations.

<u>Table of Contents</u>

Preface

Nap is your typical Midwestern city. The weather changes depending on how Mother Nature is feeling that day. There's at least one basketball court on each street, and unfortunately, some members of the white community still have a superiority complex mindset. Indianapolis, Indiana is also my hometown. Now before you turn another page of this book, it's important that you know a few things. These words are genuinely derived from a young black man in America, whose only wish is to open the eyes of those who are asleep. The people who don't understand why black people are so frustrated. My words do not represent the entire African American race; we are all extremely creative, talented and determined in different ways. We have evolving minds that are composed of brilliant thoughts and ideas. Even with that being said, some people in the black community do not understand the deep systems of oppression that we live under in America. These are the ones that you refer to when they say, "I'm not racist, I have a black friend."

So, white people, I've come to speak to you. Both the ones who feel they understand and have no biases towards black people and the ones who want nothing more than for us to just leave this country. Society was created to keep us separate so that the unequal balance of power can stay in place. If we grew up amongst one another, we would have a much better understanding of one another. But as a result of the division, you only know what you have been taught. Even though you tend to be culture appropriators, you still truly do not know the rest of us. We have more than proven we belong here but here we are, still arguing for equal rights. We're so magical, we understand our culture and yours as well. We have no choice but to be immersed in your world and until now, have had to live under your rules. Meanwhile, black people are still misunderstood because how could one understand someone they have never communicated with? I am so passionate about the possibilities we can all achieve just if we understand one another. Only communication can lead to an understanding of the way we think, learn and form opinions.

My goal is not to ignite racial wars or continue to perpetuate the negative state of race relations, but to come to you all, as humbly as I know how and explain my experiences and exactly how I feel being a black Man in America. Something that you will truly not understand until you sit down and listen and even then, it's completely possible you never will. In my work within education, a topic I regularly preach to the kids is effective communication. If you don't know, or don't care to know where someone else is coming from, you're stagnating your growth as a human and hindering any progress in humanity. I am here because I don't want you to be that person.

For so long, race has been a sensitive subject. It has now evolved into our nation's leaders flooding our timelines daily with insensitive material. Cell phone footage of black people being shot on camera by a public institution that was created to keep us in check. As a result, racial tensions are always on our mind. The created idea of race has always been a passing thought in the mind of most of us of this generation, but not always at the forefront.

I do not claim to have all the answers or even some of them. But I hope that the stories of myself and others that you will experience in this book will at least spark conversation, which I believe will consequently bring out the answers we all so desperately need. I want everyone around every water cooler in every break-room across America to ask those hard-hitting questions that will lead to a better understanding of others. I want white students in college to understand where that one black person in their class comes from, or at least be courageous enough to ask him or her. White people, please open your minds, grab a cup of coffee and take a journey through the eyes of a black man who spends his life trying not to become the next hashtag on the internet.

I would like to thank everyone who was involved in this dream of mine which is to challenge myself and those around me. I just want to leave the world a better place for my future children and yours too. To Ava DuVernay, thank you for being bold and expressing your art in a way that brings attention to the mass incarceration of black Men in America through the "13th" documentary. You're doing yourself an injustice if you haven't seen it yet. To Mary McClendon, my grandmother who is the unmovable stone in our family. Your words will live with me forever. To all the rest of my friends and family who are surprised that I decided to write a book, thank you for inspiring me to be better. You all inspire me more than you could possibly know. To all the brave people to give my book a chance, your open-mindedness is contagious. I hope that once you turn the last page of this book, you will have a greater understanding of the position black America is placed in, voluntarily and involuntarily. Let's all come together and be the change because our future generation depends on us, and we can't let them down, can we?

I.

Our Families Are Just Different

"Let somebody touch my mama
Touch my sister, touch my woman
Touch my daddy, touch my niece
Touch my nephew, touch my brother
You should chip a nigga, then throw the blower in his lap
Matter fact, I'm 'bout to speak at this convention
Call you back!"

-Kendrick Lamar (XXX)

To the brave white people who picked up this book, I want you to think about how your life would have been if you were born a different race. If you spent your entire life filling in the African American bubble instead of the white one on biased standardized tests. For the first time, these tests would not be built based on your life and opinions, but on that of the societal superior race. These are, for the most part, still required for college entry. You're saying, we must adopt your culture to earn an education. Educated black people are the most threatening to your societal hierarchy. So, there's that, but we'll expand on that later.

What if you actually grew up saying the word nigga in front of black people instead of just around your friends who look like you, or while singing along to rap songs? Well, we'll touch on that later as well. What if you grew up and wasn't able to sit in a car parked by the side of the road without attracting suspicion? What if your mom always told you to take your hood down before leaving the house, so you don't seem like a threat, or worse, get killed? What about walking into a gas station late at night and an individual with a different skin color than yours warily watches your every step? These are just a few scenarios that we as black people typically have to face. Even I, at my thin 5'9" frame, know that I can be seen as a threat. Which is funny because I'm not sure I even know how to fight, don't try me though.

The journey through these pages will break down what it has meant to myself, and some others to be black in America and how we can work together to make actual improvements. It's funny to me how in a country that prides itself on Ivy Leagues and innovation, ignorance is our greatest hurdle. A lot of you tend to not have a clue about where I come from, why I think the way I do, or why I dress a certain way nor even care to know. I don't think a lot of you care that my heart sinks to my stomach when I see a police car anywhere in my vicinity. You may not have a clue why I use the slang that I use, or why I can dunk a basketball and make it look so simple –at least I can on NBA 2k but we're not here to discuss that.

The bottom line is, we don't know one another, therefore we can't understand one another, and, well, you know what happens next. We become two groups of people who exist together but can't co-exist. We become a nation that tweets our frustrations but never look for resolutions. An open mind is a key to progression and the days of tip-toeing around these issues are gone.

My plan is to unmask completely my life as a black man and brainstorm solutions that anyone can implement with a little effort. I'm here to be very open and honest with you because there's a part of me that still believes some of you can digest the unequal realities and help us fix it. At the end of the day, everyone benefits from existing among creative and brilliant black people who have the same opportunities as their white counterparts. You all enjoy so much of our culture, but you try to prevent our minds from being explored. We have things still uncreated. Our country isn't as technologically advanced as it should be because black minds start out on the ground under a boot of injustice.

I'm here to give you my black millennial point of view of this world that we are walking into as adults. I'm just someone who invests my life into molding the youth in every way I can. Frederick Douglass was right when he said, "It's easier to build strong children than repair broken men." Today, we are sitting down at a table and opening all lines of communication. All fences separating our neighborhoods are being jumped, and I hope, if we do this right, we may just be able to live together on one accord. We're not demanding for special treatment in this country; we want the boost that you all get. That's all, and we'll definitely make it happen, but the problem is a lot of you know that but are afraid of what we'd do with our opportunities. My purpose is to bring you into my world for a second, give you a glimpse into my mind which has had the pleasure of having a vast number of experiences even as a young adult.

To understand me, you must first understand the family I come from. My parents are not married but my father is from Virginia, and my mother was born and raised in Indianapolis. Even though the South is where most of my ancestors were enslaved, Indiana is still a conservative state that the KKK still operates in. A certain high ranking government official previously served as the Indiana Governor. That should give you an indication of the way of life there. Trust me though; we will not be discussing him or his boss much throughout this text. As a child in my family– like most other African American homes, you are taught to obey your elders by any means. It really wasn't even a thought for me honestly. I think for a lot of black people, we saw how hard our single mothers worked while many of our fathers were locked up, killed, or simply never came around.

In my case, talking back or disobeying was never an option, and when I did make the wrong decision, I was swiftly brought the right way, by whatever was lying around at the moment. I was never hurt though– let me make that clear. They would tell me afterward, "boy ain't nothin wrong with you." That's funny now that I think about it. You just smacked my bare skin with leather, but ok. They were right though; I was fine. Word spread like wildfire among my mom, aunts, cousins and whichever family member who was willing to hear how Marc messed up that day. I didn't get in trouble much because I realized early on that life was better when I just did what I was supposed to do. For the longest time, though, I never understood why my mom was so eager to go run her mouth to her brothers and sisters. Like mom, can we keep this one between us? My two younger siblings and I grew up and got into disagreements with our parents, but I didn't like losing privileges or physical discipline, so I just stayed in my lane. You stayed out of "grown folk's business," and are always ready to drop everything and run when your name is called. That's just how it was, and still is for a lot of the black people I know. That's why we are so baffled when we see a white girl on Dr. Phil raising her voice at her mom, and worse cursing her parents out. When I went over to a friend's house, the expectations were intensified. We were expected to be on our best behavior. If I wasn't, those parents would tell my mom, and I'd get in more trouble than I did when I disobeyed my own parents.

Our mothers are at times the only adult we have in the house. My mom was the last of nine children, and she absorbed all ways of life from my legendary grandparents and her eight older siblings. She was the fun bouncy baby of the group who got her way much more than her siblings I'm sure. She's also very beautiful, smart and hard working. Taking nothing from my dad or any of the dads out there, but I watched my mom go without food sometimes so we could eat. I watched her be Superwoman and take us to work with her when she was working overtime to earn a little extra cash. I watched her, unfortunately, go without things she needed so that we could open at least one thing on Christmas day. I watched her sit up with us all night after working all day so that we could have a shoulder to cry on when we experienced heartache. My mom was there to make oatmeal just the way I like, with apples, cinnamon, and a little extra milk so it won't be too thick after I come inside from the shoveling the driveway. Even though I didn't agree with everything she said or did, she gave me the best gift, an opportunity to lead a life down a different and better path. She made an ultimate sacrifice and allowed me to move in with my uncle and aunt to obtain better opportunities. My mom is so magical, she created a family out of a broken one. She loves us with all her heart, and we love her too. The black woman is truly a treasure not only to African Americans but the human race in general and salute to every single one of them.

Let me give an instance of my mom's love for me in one scenario. It happened during my sophomore year in high school, my grades were dropping– I was very rarely a straight A student, but I got B's and an occasional C. It was my second high school at that point and, to be honest, I probably should have stayed at the first. It was at Arsenal Technical High School where I had received all A's and B's and laid a good academic foundation for my high school education. Tech is a public school located outside downtown Indianapolis. After my first semester, my mom and I decided to switch schools. I just wasn't comfortable there and figured I would have a better experience at a school closer to my neighborhood where I already had a good number of friends.

Financially, things were becoming even harder for us than they were before. My mom, like way too many black mothers, was a single one for most of my childhood. First, that's not easy for anyone with three children. It's natural to look at the faults of my mom and say she should have done better, but no one knows her heart like I do. She cared about nothing but making sure her babies were taken care of. I had slept the last few years on my grandparent's couch because there wasn't enough bedrooms or beds to accommodate my grandparents, my younger sister, my new baby brother, my mom, and the occasional aunt or uncle. So, as the odd man out, I had to make those sacrifices. I was now attending Arlington High School on the east side of Indianapolis where I can still only remember one white student in the entire school.

The culture of black kids in the inner city and beyond really is typically filled with roasting your friends just as bad, if not worse than you roast your enemies. We bond by telling jokes at one another's expense, and we're very good at it. Not only are we clever in that regard, but we also know that roasting is a part of life and we take the jokes better than others. More specifically, I was raised doing this from the very beginning, so I was able to hold my own at the lunch table. It got me out of a lot of situations that could have turned out badly. There were fights in and outside the school every week, mainly because students represented different hoods around the school, and also because there wasn't a lot of teaching going on. Depending on what neighborhood you were from, those kids were your teammates in a sense. You rode the bus together and protected one another for the most part. I try to be realistic and I knew that claiming my hood wasn't the life for me. I've always been small framed, and I never learned how to fight. I just joked my way out of tight corners and was able to befriend people from every hood in the school. We're so creative that we've created a social battleground to bring us together. If you can make others laugh, you're good to go. For those of you reading who feel like you may want to try roasting the black guy who sits next to you at work, don't. Black people have the sense of family a lot of times. You have to be invited to participate in our activities like that. If you intrude without representation, don't be surprised when the whole family comes after you.

Clearly, I was doing more roasting, than I was doing school work. We were pretty wild, and now that I work in Education, I realize we gave those poor teachers more than they could handle, so some decided not to. There's such a disconnection in a lot of our schools because none of the teachers or administrators look like us. Therefore, it's difficult to build trust among students and teachers but it's essential to every child's success. These are people from two different worlds coming together. One side is there to help but has no clue what the child's life is like outside school hours. The other side is bombarded by distractions and is frustrated because the teacher doesn't understand them. The school curriculum is framed around norms that are custom for you and you only. There are rarely any connectors that link, a black student with the material they are learning. I was no exception to this trend. My grades started to drop because handling my business in the classroom became less and less of a priority. There were fights every day and distractions everywhere. School was more of a fashion show than a place students came to learn. A lot of staff didn't seem to care about anything we did. There seemed to be no level of trust amongst the staff and us. They were there to do their jobs, and we were there because we had to be.

It was my mom who chose to swallow her pride and realize that my uncle could offer me opportunities than she could at the time. Moving in with my uncle provided life necessities like a bed, a bedroom, and a safe comfortable environment. My mom, being the courageous and selfless woman that she is, never complained about it but I could tell it ate away at her. There is one hope I have to this day, I hope I live my life in a way that makes her feel like her decision was worth it. She sent me to live with my uncle, his wife, and her two children in a more stable home, I went to a much better school in a better school system on the edge of the city. Meaning, the school was roughly 30% white unlike the other with a white boy here or there in the back of the classroom not saying a word. This to me was a "white" school. Not only were there white students, but the school had a pool and more than two options in the school lunch line. The teachers, for the most part, seemed to care if their students reached college or not, and college was preached throughout the halls every day.

This eventually helped me straighten up and take my education seriously because I too wanted to get out and make something of my life. Being around positive influences and kids who had dreams of going to college had a great influence on me. Before this point, I knew that college was the best option for my life but I never seriously figured out how I would get there. As kids in their house, we didn't want for anything. All we had to focus on was school which was a huge relief. Even though my Uncle Allen and Aunt Vanessa's expectations were high, they took away all those distractions that were floating around my home and high school and what do you know, I was able to graduate on time and eventually made my way to college. I was afforded the opportunity that others in my neighborhood didn't have. Who knows, if they had the same chances I did, that your children do, we might have the cure for cancer by now. It takes a very strong woman to do that, and my heroic black mother did that for me, in which I am truly thankful.

My family has always been pretty tight-knit and parents passing down ways to survive in America as a black man were part of natural conversation. From a very young age, I was taught that my "A" in school had to be an "A+" because white America already expected my life to play out in a certain way. According to some, I'm either supposed to sell drugs and go to prison, or sell drugs and land in the cemetery prematurely. It makes me laugh when I have to soften my approach in some encounters with you all because you tend to assume I'll get angry or violent at your first wrong move. First, I can't go to prison because I like regular food too much. Even If I am lucky enough to survive any of those expected paths, I'm either dribbling a basketball or passing my mixtape out to anyone who is willing to take it. I didn't have parents who were buoyant enough to build up a huge college fund for me from birth. My family didn't have connections in high places to get me into an elite private school or get me my first job out of college. When you live in an environment where everyone is struggling for the same basic things, your mind is limited to what you see.

We are influenced by the media almost as much as you are, so when the only successful black people we see on the television is playing sports or rapping, we don't think about much else. We typically don't have uncles who are Wall Street bankers. We don't have many aunts who are attorneys. So naturally, we gravitate towards what we know to be possible. Do you see the difference here? This is what continues the cycle of poverty and entrapment. For sure some of this is our fault. We don't seek out new opportunities to make a better life for ourselves, but in reality, what kid doesn't? Our schools don't teach us that there is more than one way to cut a cookie. So, when a white person tells us to pull ourselves up by our bootstraps, they fail to realize that we don't have the bootstraps let alone know how to pull ourselves up. We have to find those bootstraps first, which sometimes take years into adulthood before we actually find them. These are reasons that I knew I had to outperform my white peers who already had the stable foundation to set themselves up for success in their lives. Putting this into perspective, if you didn't grow up seeing your friends make snacks out of bread, sugar and cinnamon, you won't know what to eat when there isn't a pantry full of all the snacks you could ever dream of. If you didn't grow up hearing stories of parents who put bills in their children's names to dodge debt and bad credit, you wouldn't know that's even a possibility.

We learned how to survive in these abandoned neighborhoods. We have all the bad streets in our communities, including Dr. Martin Luther King Jr. Blvd., that's ironically in the hood in every city. Some of you can't even stand to drive on a street named after one of this country's greatest leaders because he's black. Instead of regularly flying to beaches to relax, we have our local parks that are also ignored by our city. When we see police ride down our street, we are ready to protect ourselves instead of feeling protected. Our streets are stained with oil because the cars we drive are on their last leg. A lot of us don't have air conditioning in our homes so we are forced outside to live amongst one another.

Everyone's dollars are so crucial to them that when there is a disagreement regarding money, that's where a lot of altercations come in. We get paid less than you do for doing the same job, so to survive, we have to find our side hustle to stay afloat. Kids in your neighborhood aren't worried about their lights being shut off so they are able to focus on more youthful things. Survival mode is nonstop, so of course we confuse you by our mentality because you've most likely never been in our shoes.

Ideas

1. Our families want us to succeed just as much as your families want you to and possibly even more. Whatever we do, if we incorporate the families of black people, it can be a motivating factor to do well. If you require families to be involved when you are rehabilitating someone in prison that could possibly push their progression. So, what about building a program where a family member can come monitor the inmate's progression? Give them motivation to effectively rehabilitate themselves. If the inmates do well in whatever skill they are learning or degree that they are pursuing, they can potentially get lighter sentences.

2. On the same token, when dealing with black people, you have to understand our family. You have to understand where we come from. Ask your black co-worker about their family. How does their family impact them? Ask them about what their friends mean to them. If you do all this correctly, you'll realize that you have more in common than you may think. Then you realize that you can accomplish

more together than you can separately. Employers can implement "get to know you," hours for their staff. Maybe all staff members meet one on one with one of their colleagues each week. You have a set of talking points and it's just a chance to get to know one another. They would then rotate every week and meet with a different colleague until they have met with everyone. This includes the CEO (at least reasonably) and the custodians.

II.

Makin' Somethin' Outta Nothin'

"Far from a Harvard student, Just had the balls to do it."

-Jay Z (What More Can I Say)

Contrary to the stereotype that black people are lazy, there are, and I actually know a lot of hard-working black men and women. I quickly learned that whatever I wanted, I had to go out and get it. Excuses were only going to keep me from changing my life for the better. At the age of 12, I ordered free business cards off the internet, filled the lawn mower up with gas and walked around my neighborhood asking to cut my neighbors' grass. I went door to door all summer and left my cards around the neighborhood. I even gave some out at church too. My grandfather would let me load the mower into his trunk, and he'd take me to my appointments with my customers. I knew my mom would do everything she could to get me the things I needed, but I was on my own when it came to things I wanted. Like a new BMX trick bike with all the accessories including four pegs on the tires. I knew that if I wanted anything, I was going to have to get it myself. Even as a preteen, I knew the financial circumstances I lived under. I knew my mom had just enough to pay the rent, put food in our mouths and gas in the car. I didn't even feel right asking mom for anything because I knew she simply did not have it. I didn't want to make her feel any worse than she possibly already did.

I did well for myself that summer, and I was very proud. It felt good having a few dollars in my pocket. It also felt good being able to help my mom out, here and there. I had been the man of the house for a while at that point so helping out where I could felt like a responsibility. I started working early because I couldn't even spell allowance, let alone ask for it. I was also able to grab me a couple Platinum Fubu outfits for the new school year. I had to stay fresh by any means necessary. I bought all types of things with my money. If only I was given some financial wisdom on how to save my money and reinvest it, I would be in a totally different position today, 15 years later. If you can imagine, both my mom and I had no idea how to handle our money.

We had never thought of the concept of saving. If we had it, we could spend it. This lack of knowledge is the main thing that keeps us behind, generation after generation. We are not only starting with nothing, but the education required to pull ourselves out of financial grief is being withheld from us. I'm still battling the consequences of the financial mistakes I made in the past. I still don't fully understand everything today. I took it upon myself to learn about assets and how to build wealth. I now know what financial seeds I will plant in my children.

Once I turned 14, I got my first job at Staples. At the time, minimum wage was like $5.50 per hour, I was making $7. I was making about $100 a week, and you couldn't convince me that I wasn't making Oprah Winfrey's money. As the oldest child, I wanted to be able to take as much pressure off my mom as I could. I was constantly worried about being a burden that I just knew that I had to provide for myself. I say this to let you know that a lot of times in the African American community, we have to grow up really fast. We are forced into the world of adulthood due to our circumstances. This is what I mean when I say African Americans in this country are not born with some of the privileges that our white counterparts are born with. A lot of times, I was more worried about making money to survive than I was about my homework. This sets us up for life to focus on doing whatever it takes to survive. Like my mom, many single mothers become magicians when trying to provide for their children. Unfortunately, this mindset can often lead to finding illegal sources of income without any remorse. It's a 'do what you have to do' mentality. Our survival instincts are unmatched because we have had to make a way out of no way since we were brought over in the belly of slave ships. When The System makes it so hard for us to get a job, it's no wonder why we land in jail and with a record. Once those felonies start piling up, then it is next to impossible to obtain a legal source of income that we can use to provide for our families.

In reality, drug dealers do the same thing that prescription drug companies do—just on a smaller scale, but the white man's method of selling drugs does not criminalize them but glorifies them as business masterminds. Their business has a negative effect on the people purchasing their product, but the seller sets themselves up for financial freedom. Instead, we are thrown in prison at much faster rates than anyone else. There should be a rehabilitating system in prison once prisoners get out to provide them with the education needed to navigate their journey of rejoining society. I'm talking real programs too, not underfunded programs that are created just to make The System look good. An inmate sitting in a cell for 23 hours a day does nothing to help the inmate change their life but deteriorates their mind to the point of prison life is all they know or are comfortable with.

No child should have to worry about what they are going to eat for dinner or if the lights will be on when they get home. Especially in a country that brags about being the most powerful country in the world. We aren't powerful until we start helping the minorities in our urban communities. We aren't powerful until, every child in the country is fed and nourished. We aren't powerful until our students' quality of education is the same no matter what neighborhood they live in. We aren't powerful until everyone's life is held in the highest regard. This way, more will be done when an officer takes the life on a black person. We are bombarded with consumerism ads that paint an inaccurate reality of what we should do with our money. A child's adolescence should be spent on building those personal skills and learning as much as they can in school, stress-free. I am not saying The System causes these issues, we as black people bring some of this on ourselves, like all humans do. Mass incarceration already takes enough black fathers out of the home. We don't have to contribute to it by being deadbeats and walking out of our children's lives. At the same time, I truly feel the black man is under attack and being a convicted felon strips away so many opportunities that even after being released from prison, it becomes hard for a man to provide for his children. We were taught that we had to use our survival skills to make it to the next day because this country does not care about us. If you feel differently, allow me go a little deeper.

As a black man, I pose a threat to you when I walk into a store late at night, or when I'm walking down the street. I live in a nice building full of condos, and when someone is about to get on the elevator, I have to stand up straight and smile so that I look less intimidating. A lot of times, I can feel the sense of fear coming from a white woman. I've never hurt a fly and have dodged fights my whole life except that one crazy day in middle school. Instead, it's me who tries to not come off as a super predator as someone referred to us as in the past. A simple item of clothing such as a hooded sweatshirt sets off the alarms in some people's heads as soon as they see me in one, even though all types of people wear hoodies every day. When I sense that a white person may be in fear, I have to make my voice slightly higher to let whoever know that I come in peace. We call it our white voice. We use it when we code switch. Even in my workplace, and I'm sure a lot of black people will agree when I say this, but I can't communicate comfortably like I would at home or around my friends and family. I'm not referring to any vulgarity, but I have to code switch and speak in a way that you are familiar with. White people, if you are confused about what I mean, "crib" is a common term used in the black community when referring to one's home. When at work or in public, I know not to use the term so that I am not viewed as uneducated or unprofessional, though that is the true language I use when I'm comfortable. Professionalism and being professional doesn't take into account how black people communicate and what makes us comfortable. Even the idea of "professionalism" is completely biased and used to make us more like you. Instead, it's always our job to make you all comfortable. All you see is people who look like you. Think about what your workplace does to make African Americans feel welcome and comfortable. If you think that you aren't able to be yourself at work, try to imagine what it's like for us.

There is something I am aware of in every single encounter with a white person. On the weekends, I drive for Uber which is interesting because it forces white people to trust that I will get them to their destination safely. This also requires an extreme code switch because some people are already apprehensive about getting into stranger's cars regardless of race or gender. White people have asked me all types of questions to ensure that I am legit. I know for a fact they wouldn't ask some of those same questions if I was a white driver. A white woman has even asked me about my license plates and registration, thinking I wouldn't notice what she was trying to say. I've also had riders suddenly decide they will "wait and get a different Uber" upon seeing me pull up. That young lady was willing to pay the unnecessary cancellation fee rather than take the chance of getting into the car with a black man. I drive a six-year-old stock Chevy Cruze, and I have had a white man ask me, "How'd did you go about getting such a nice car?" Man, my car is not that nice, I just keep it clean. I think the worst part of it all is that I am not surprised when any of these situations arise. These types of encounters and a lot worse encounters have been the norm for us for generations. You have to understand that being a black man comes with certain assumptions about me before I even open my mouth. If all you know about me is the color of my skin, you know nothing about me at all.

Ideas

1. Why don't we give our poor kids a constructive way to earn responsible good money and learn some skills along the way

2. What if the city put different projects under the direction of young people? The new park downtown needs a design? Find a local high school student from a lower income neighborhood to earn the position. Give him or her the team around them so that they can see it through. Watch the kid flourish. This helps the kid because this gives them the experience of being a project leader and a way to work hard and be compensated for it. The community gets a revamp and forward-thinking design for a park for a lower price than paying a professional. When the kids invest in the community, they will be less likely to tear it down.

3. It is going to take a long time for people to eliminate the automatic assumptions that they have about other people. If we start now, we can change the minds of generations to come. If you can teach people about the cultures of people across the water, you can teach them about the cultures here in America. The way black people dress is a part of our culture-from our ancestors down to the current generation. Don't let our effort to be comfortable by wearing baggy clothes, strike fear in your heart when you see us. Most times, it's just the culture.

III.

College Dropout

"Man I promise, she's so self-conscious
She has no idea what she doin' in college
That major that she majored in don't make no money
But she won't drop, her parents'll look at her funny
Now, tell me that ain't insecurr
The concept of school seems so securr
Sophomore, three yurrs, aint picked a carurr
She like, "Fuck it, I'll just stay down hurr and do hair."

Kanye West (All Falls Down)

It has been an ongoing battle in the black community for equitable educational opportunities. To be completely honest, I am sick and tired of the government spending money everywhere but in public, more specifically urban schools. White people, please listen when I say, to have equal opportunity, you must have an equal opportunity to education. Now please do not get me wrong, a person must first want it for themselves, but with so many roadblocks in the way, some may feel it's better to take the easier, sometimes illegal, route to feed themselves and their family. The odds are stacked against us to make it out of our situations, so a lot of us decide to take our chances. When Ronald Reagan put crack into black neighborhoods, he had two goals, to rip families apart by sending black men to prison and get us addicted to a drug that tears our lives apart. He exceeded his goals, and the affects still linger to this day. Do you realize that he brought the drugs into the neighborhood and then had his wife start the Just say no campaign? I feel disrespected that he would try to flip it on us like we went to Columbia to get the cocaine ourselves.

To take it a step further, like always, we were criminalized to an extraordinary extent. I, as a black man am still much more likely to go to jail than you or your children. I'm not here to bash you because I find no joy in that. But for us all to progress, we all have to face reality. The reality is, this country was built on our backs and still tries to keep us on our backs. Believe it or not white people, you all do not know everything. You know everything from your viewpoint. When people say we are lazy and don't want to get jobs, that is not always the case. I almost don't blame people for not wanting a job that they have to go into every day and are forced to assimilate to your culture. Obviously, you all don't feel comfortable in ours so you have to understand how we may feel.

It has become more and more common for job applicants to need a college education and experience to even be considered for a role. The way our education system is set up, you get the best education as a child if your parents have a lot of money. This does not include just private schools either because if parents have a little bit of money, they will most likely live in better neighborhoods that have more money to dedicate to education via their taxes. Do you really think that since a child grows up poor, they don't deserve the same education your son or daughter does? It's a very simple formula that some of you do not understand because you haven't experienced living in a poor neighborhood with underperforming schools. Yet people still call us lazy and allude that depend on social services. When in actuality, you all depend on it just as much as we do.

In my opinion, poor schools inhabit uninspired teachers who do more harm to students than good at times. Teachers have one of the most difficult jobs in our country. They serve in one of the most important roles, but get paid as if they aren't needed. It takes a lot of heart and patience to be a teacher, especially in an underfunded school.

In high performing schools, as a parent, you take certain things for granted. The facilities take a hit, year after year in poor neighborhoods. Not only does the school's appearance take a hit, but you can't guarantee that there is always going to be air conditioning. Supplies become much more precious, and something as essential as paper towels can run out. Yes, I've experienced this before. Grass grows to levels so high, students aren't able to play and therefore don't get essential exercise. Yes, I've experienced this as well. What about when a teacher quits right before the school year starts because they can't survive off a teacher's income where they live. I've seen a 3rd-grade class go without a teacher for almost an entire semester. Then there's also the very common leaks in classrooms that have short-term fixes and interrupt the learning process.

Just last year, Detroit public schools had wild mushrooms growing in their classrooms. You'd think how would they let it get that bad. With these distractions, a teacher must still be able to gain the trust of each student, even when they have a class of 35 kids. This must happen before they can properly help the students learn. When white teachers are placed in black schools and don't come in with an open mind to get to know the students, the teacher is not looking to succeed. We've all heard the stories about teachers telling students that they won't make it in life but what about the teachers who don't say anything at all? What about the teachers who are tenured and just show up to receive their salary and benefits? Those examples are just as detrimental to the futures of these black students as the teachers who under mind students' potential.

As a sophomore in high school, I was attending my second school in two years, which was the all black one I mentioned earlier. I had a particular world history class that is cemented in my brain forever. This was the typical class in the school that everyone had to take and knew what it was going to be like before they even walked in on the first day. Mr. McAllister, a gray-haired white gentleman, had been teaching at the school for decades and was pretty comfortable in his role. He was never disrespectful or rude in any way, but he was not there because he cared about us. I may go as far as to say; he did not prepare us to further our education. For the sake of the story though, I'll say that's not the case. I feel as though he had given up hope for us.

Throughout the year, I can count on one hand how many times he got up in front of us and addressed the class. He never held conversations with us; he never asked how our day was going or how our moms were doing. He never looked to get to know us past our last name. He knew nothing about our lives and what went on after we walked out of his class each day. Anyone in education knows that these are foundational steps to help build those important relationships with students. None of that took place the entire semester. He would write our book assignment on the board and sit down at his desk to read the newspaper, every single day. If we had a question, he might answer it, but that was all.

Black education is taken as a joke in this country, and I am really tired of it. There is no reason he should have still had his job if he wasn't going to do it. Obviously, this would often lead to an out of control classroom which totally wastes everyone's time. Mr. McAllister was a good man, but I feel as though if he taught in a wealthier neighborhood, at a school that paid very well and people were fighting to get enrolled, he would have kept teaching. If he had a classroom full of white students he was already comfortable and familiar with, he would have kept teaching. If Mr. McAllister had just a little bit of care for us, he would have kept teaching. Instead, he decided that the personal satisfaction he got from reading his newspaper every day was more important. Year after year, he sent another set of unprepared black students into the real world. He killed their confidence to apply for college because they felt unprepared. He told a group of black students, without verbalizing it, that their education wasn't important. So, there was no reason to take it seriously. He didn't care about us. He had this very noble profession and did nothing with it. He had the future of America in his hands and could care less if we made something out of ourselves. But yet, his neighbors, friends, and family will be the ones telling us to take advantage of the same opportunities white students have been given, well, we would if we had them. With this going on, I'm sure Mr. McAllister was still getting a hearty pat on the back because he went to work at a school in the ghetto to educate black kids.

This is why our parents tell us that every "A" we receive needs to be an "A+". We grow up thinking that we have to be much better than the white student who has been molded and prepared to succeed in school and adulthood. Black parents depend so much on the teachers and the schools because their time is spent at work and dealing with the prejudices at their workplace. Many black collegiate students are still first-generation college students who have no clue how to navigate getting there, much more making it through. Black students still tend to work with old technology at school and are being left behind by their counterparts here in places like Silicon Valley. All the essentials that your white students use is not widely available for all students, believe it or not. This limits the options students have when it comes to how they learn. Everyone doesn't learn the same way, and when you lack funds, it makes it harder to help students who don't connect with the standard way of learning. If we spent more money on training our teachers to teach effectively, at least they would be more equipped to work with what they have. But, the combination of low resources and inadequate teachers is deadly and fails underserved kids every year. Students in wealthier neighborhoods tend to have healthier options than the frozen prepackaged foods that they heat up every day in underfunded schools. So, you tell me how a black student has the same opportunity as white ones. With these factors that were designed to work against us, it is little wonder why our interest in school drops as we matriculate through the public-school system.

By now we all know how expensive college tuition is. My education during my four years at Indiana University cost me close to $90,000. My mother makes a little over a third of that. Luckily, I did qualify for the 21st Century Scholars Program in Indiana. For those that are unfamiliar, if you fall under a certain income and maintain a certain grade point average through high school, the state will pay for your tuition if you attend a state school. Now, my mom had the wherewithal to seek out these opportunities as early as 8th grade. So, I did have it better than most when it came to paying for school. I was a poor kid who grew up on the east side of Indianapolis. I was given an opportunity and have made the best of it ever since. Though this program was a great tool in getting low-income students into school, it still never reached nearly enough students in poverty.

This alone is enough for students of color to be discouraged from applying for college. It's as simple as this; you need money to receive an education. To have that kind of money, you either have to dig tediously for options to pay for school like I did, your parents have to be able to afford it, or have a high enough credit score to apply for college loans. These tend to be rare in the low-income communities where a lot of our black students reside. Of course, there are scholarships and grants out there to assist with these payments, but then again, you have to know how to find them. You need the resources to be able to find them. You need counselors and teachers who care about you to pass along any information that they may have concerning them. You need parents who are in the home long enough to push the students. What about the students who don't have a computer or Wi-Fi at home? Then they need a ride to the library because it's too far a distance to actually be able to get a lot accomplished there. You also need access to individuals who have gone through the process before. For those that feel I'm making excuses, I'd like to see you grow up with these scenarios and see how far you get. I'm saying this because you may not have even thought about any of this before.

It's easy to judge if you've never lived in someone else's shoes. With so much working against a child, it's easy to revert to what you see every day and lose hope. A lot of us are told from a very young age that we will wind up dead or in jail. As a black man, it pains me even to type that but it is true, and we have heard it so many times before. So, when that mindset is instilled in you at a young age, it's hard to let that go. We, as in all Americans, instead of letting young black males know how hard it is to get to college, ask them which college they will be attending. When neither of your parents was able to make it, it becomes much harder to offset that precedent.

Surviving college is an entirely different battle, one which I saw many of my black peers lose to many times. In college, as I'm sure many of you know, those scholarships that you may have been lucky enough to receive for your freshman year can run out. Those loan companies may stop lending money. It's a common theme to be broke in college. But the common theme amongst African American students can be that there is no one to call at home to send you some money when you need it. A lot of us were on our own when it came to getting money for necessities. Now mind you, a lot of us grew up in a single parent home. Remember those superhero black mothers I was talking about? Well, even they can only do so much. So, what happens when money has run out, and mom needs you to send her some just as much as you need the same from her? If you're anything like me, you got a job. Sometimes even two to make ends meet. Now, I am not saying that only black students get jobs in college. I will say that we get them more so because we have to rather than because we want to. I think students who work during college are commendable. To me, it shows commitment and drive to make the best for yourself. The only problem is, you're working to earn a degree so that you can get a good job to pay for that degree.

It's a cycle that, when looked at closely, doesn't seem to add up. Too many Millennials, in general, came out of college with a mortgage-sized loan before they even got a job. We as a country should be investing as many resources into education so that we in return have an abundance of citizens who can positively contribute to their communities. There's no reason to me why students should be financially punished for wanting to expand their knowledge on a certain topic. College is not easy, and if it were, everyone would go. So, it is never the best thing to add extra responsibilities to those that are pursuing a degree. Instead of committing your time to your studies, you have to go clock in at work. This can lead to falling behind in school and an assortment of other challenges. It's just another obstacle that a lot of my black peers and I have to endure. College costs continue to climb and the next time you hear of an increase, just think about those black 18-year-old kids whose college dreams disappear every year.

White people, I'm just here to communicate to you some common challenges that we face generation after generation after generation. Believe me, we will always have work to do on our end to get our kids to college, but we don't need the extra unnecessary burdens that our white peers don't even see. Getting into college is only the first step. Surviving is another. Race relations in our country is as bad as they have ever been in my lifetime. College campuses are where teenage kids, transform into young adults. These are where true values and morals are formed. Kids are on their own for the first time and can make their own decisions. This is also the time when racism shows its ugly little peanut head. Indiana University was the first place I noticed that this country was built by people who look like me but not for people who look like me. Everything about the campus is to make white students feel comfortable. From the slavery murals on the wall in lecture halls to overabundance of white faculty.

I wholeheartedly appreciate the Black Culture Centers on college campuses around the country but the fact that we need them shows that these institutions are not for us. It's almost like the institution gives you this small part of the campus to go to and feel comfortable. That's at least when you all aren't defacing it with racial slurs. If you all really cared about us, you would incorporate our culture into every aspect of the institution right next to the representations of your culture. I'm speaking for all minorities that are marginalized on the edge of campus. Stop putting us off to the side so that white students can feel comfortable everywhere else on campus. It takes a white person being uncomfortable for them to see actually what's going on around them. Maybe then you will understand our plight and be inspired to use some of your privileged resources to help steer us towards equality. Confederate statues stand proudly on hilltops, and we are expected to just walk past it like it's not there. Teach your children that black people are capable of making it to college the same way you all are. We aren't accepted to colleges just to raise the black representation because if that were the case, we'd make up more than 3% of the student population at predominantly white institutions. For me, I encountered the true power of the white race on the very first day I stepped on to campus my freshman year in the fall of 2009.

Like the average 18-year-old kid, I got to campus and was ready to do most of what it had to offer. I had watched how fun college was on television, and I knew that my time had come. At IU, 'welcome week' is your first taste of the new school year. There is always the A2Z Block Party that my fraternity brothers and I threw as a staple of guaranteed fun during the welcome week. For those that are unfamiliar, welcome week typically occurs the first-week students arrive on campus but before classes start. Every year it's an exciting time before it quickly gets very real. You can feel the excitement just by walking down the street. You see other students dressed up; The women are wearing dresses and heels, which was pretty new to me coming from high school.

The fellas may have on a nice pair of Sperry's instead of Jordan's (but trust me, Jordan's were still very prevalent) and button-up shirts. My friends and I knew that this campus wasn't going to know what hit them by the time we were through. It was time to go meet some ladies, I mean that's what college is all about right? So, we took our time and got fresh for whatever woman that was willing to give us any attention. We probably doused ourselves in cheap cologne and put our fake earrings in. For me, I had to make sure the laces in my sneakers were loose enough to look good but tight enough, so they didn't go flying off.

At that time, we were young, naive freshmen who were just out to find a good time. I'm not sure why we had forgotten everything we had ever learned in regards to dealing with white people. We felt as though since it was college, everyone got along with everyone since we were just trying to have a good time. We put our 18-year-old minds together and figured the frats were the best place to go. I'll pause there because that's when we were truly trippin. We are arguably the most prominent University in the state of Indiana. The one state in the Midwest that we can guarantee without a shadow of a doubt will go red every four years in November. This was in 2009, so we dressed the only way we knew, but our skin was still as brown as a UPS uniform. It is myself and four of my good friends; Wes, D, Mel, and Money who have gone on to do incredible things with our lives. We laughed and joked our way down frat row looking for the party that seemed to be having the most fun from the outside. I saw a house that reminded me of the scene from 'He Got Game' when Jesus went on a visit to that white school and suggested we try that one. The building simply should have had a "White's only" sign on the front because that is all we saw. It took a little negotiating at the door to gain access. I don't remember exactly what the guy at the door was asking us, but it reminded me of a job interview. We had no girls with us, and we were dressed like the starting five on a high school basketball team.

Once we were finally let in, I felt like I was in a dream. Even when we would go to the suburbs in high school to party, there would still be black people there. Here, it felt like we were the black dots on a dice. It seemed we caught everyone's eye in this huge mansion. The only attention we got from women was a mix of, who let them in here and where is my purse. I laugh now because we probably felt as unsafe, if not more unsafe than they did with us being there. That, me seeing a line of cocaine on the table, we all knew this wasn't the place for us. We were probably there for at most seven minutes. We never even got to the part where someone politely escorted us out because we made everyone uncomfortable, which is what typically happens. Whenever our presence makes you uncomfortable, we can feel it. In those instances, I typically try to make them feel comfortable by smiling or changing my speech, but I'm tired of doing that. I don't think I had ever had that feeling before. The feeling of being an unwanted outsider who was ruining a good time for a mansion full of people. After that experience, I think I only stepped into a frat house one more time in my four years at Indiana University. After that, the white people partied by themselves, and we typically did the same, aside from the few occasions we had a white friend to vouch for us. We welcomed all people at our parties and actually encouraged others to come experience college life as we knew it.

Brown vs. The Board of Education, the groundbreaking Supreme Court Case stated: "separate educational facilities are inherently unequal." After many years of attending segregated schools, students in 1954 experienced something generations before them probably never thought they'd see. Some of them would begin going to school and seeing white kids sitting at the desks. These are two polar opposite worlds clashing together at the most innocent times in a person's life, as a child. This was really powerful and for many reasons. The 'Brown vs. The Board of Education' case appeared to be a breakthrough for black education in this country. It gave hope to many black families that their children would then have the same quality education that white students had. The ruling allowed black families to dream bigger when considering their children's futures. Parents had hope that their kids would actually find a career using their brains rather than their hands. It's interesting that something some of you take for granted could be such an accomplishment in the black community. This is a clear example of the inequalities that follow us from birth.

If racism and prejudice are learned, why not require students to complete a social equality curriculum right way from the very beginning? Why is it not a core part of grade school curriculum? We have to start them young. We have the power to mold the next generation the way we would like. You would think, with oppression plaguing us since you stole this land from the Indians, we would put in systematic adjustments to improve the lives of future generations. Just think: what if all children were required to learn the accomplishments of each culture represented in the classroom? We should be teaching them communication techniques which instead of promoting separation, show them how to overcome their differences and succeed together. Teach kids what's offensive to certain cultures along with what's appreciated. This culture appreciation curriculum needs to be carried early because it's one thing that the kids will use for the rest of their lives. White kids should grow up learning about us just as we learn all about them. I got tired of learning about old white men who most likely held prejudices against my ancestors. We should all know the plight of Cesar Chavez and what he did to improve the life of many Mexicans in this country. It's not hard, but until you all come down your high horses and recognize that you need us here, it won't happen. You all, as a whole, become extremely comfortable in your own ignorance and don't realize how it is deteriorating our society. Am I sure that you all will open your eyes and combat social inequality? Not a chance. I do however have hope in the children that with the proper training, can take this country to new heights. Prejudices are embedded so deep into your veins that it would take generations to change that, and the way things are going now, I don't think we'll be here that long. I can't complain about your racism and bigotry if I'm not doing anything to change it.

I can only control what I can control, which is what I represent to my students, and how I mold my own children. I haven't brought a life into this world yet, but when I do, my child will be able to face any situation with people who look unlike them. He or she will at least know how to use their resources to find out how to best approach situations with empathy and respect. In return, this will open many more doors for my child. My child will be super successful in whatever area of life they pursue because they can work alongside anybody. Even your own cloud of oppression will be no match for my child who will change the lives of everyone around them. So, while your student sits in his or her all-white classroom not acknowledging people in this world who don't share their skin color, their connections with a diverse group of people will be limited. Just a word for the wise, it will not be long before minorities will be the majority in this country and there's nothing you can do about it but accept it and find out how you can work with us.

Now, I have to write a book explaining to you how I feel and ask them to join in the conversations to get to know us. It's pretty ridiculous since we have been in this country just as long as you have. The Netflix Documentary entitled, "13th" by Ava DuVernay inspired me to do what I could to make an impact and fight this racism. I plan to live out my goal of changing the hearts of white people one person at a time. I also want you all to know that, even though Brown won their case versus the Board of Education, the same inequality was reconfigured and still holds true to this day. Obviously, the ruling has not held up as strong as we hoped it would, but we just have it to the long list of disappointments that we already live with. Schools are still segregated, and equitable education still seems so far away.

You force schools to support themselves with the neighborhood's property taxes. To me, this is very problematic because once again, my people are typically still the poor people going to the poor schools. Children deserve the same education no matter what community they are born into. You are influencing their educational career from the day they are driven home from the hospital. Now, the schools educating the less privileged children are struggling to pay good teachers. In no way am I saying these schools don't have good teachers at all, but they face the challenge of retaining those good teachers. You are less likely to have the elaborate parent clubs in these schools and poorer neighborhoods as well. There are a lot of single-parent homes in our communities across the country. These parents are usually doing everything they can to take care of their children. They may have more pressing issues to deal with before being able to help around at their child's school. There are no stay at home moms in the hood. Using this method of funding schools with neighborhood taxes, The System still has its hand in segregating our children.

I'll be honest, you all know that my black brothers and sisters are some of the most brilliant people on this planet. I am not saying that we are better than anyone else, but we are different. We can do anything we set our minds on. You all are so worried about losing your stranglehold on the power in this country that you are willing to deprive black kids of a high-quality education. You know that we can quickly become the best in whatever we set out to do if given the opportunity. I don't agree with everything about President Obama, but you all let a black man become arguably the best President this country has ever seen. You let a young black man named Tiger Woods step on the golf course and dominate it for over a decade. Two dynamic black sisters crafted their skill on the tennis court and have become two of the most decorated tennis players in the world. I believe Serena is the best ever- man and woman, easily. Oprah Winfrey revolutionized daytime talk shows and overall entertainment. You are afraid that with a proper education, we will invent equal societal systems that are so good, even your own people will have no choice but to support it. I've said this plenty of times, and I'll say it again, it's not your power that we want. We want the power to spread amongst us, black, white, Mexican, Asian, and everyone else who makes up the melting pot of America.

The lack of quality education is not the only problem plaguing our communities. Another big problem is our health. I interviewed another one of my best friends to gain some of his insight on the topics discussed. I met Jamel in my Chemistry class during our Junior year of high school and we immediately became good friends. Jamel and I eventually went on to be roommates our freshman year of college, and after obtaining a master's degree, he is now in his second year of medical school. He always brings encouraging words to anyone who needs them. Jamel is always ready to hear you out if you ever need to vent. He sees a different aspect of injustice while working in the medicine field. He asked me, "Do you ever wonder why African Americans tend to have the worst health?" I can guarantee you that it is not always because we choose to. Our neighborhoods are riddled with greasy, cheap fast food restaurants that some of us live on our entire lives. Sometimes, there may even be more than one on the same corner. These restaurants do nothing but clog our arteries and send us down a spiral of health issues. This dynamic is so apparent that Jamel says, "I can tell you your potential lifespan, based on your zip code." This is something commonly known amongst medical professionals, but for some reason, nothing is being done about it.

When we develop lifelong health issues from the food that floods our neighborhoods, a lot of us don't have access to healthcare because our job either doesn't offer it or has co-pays that do not fit into our tight budgets. According to Jamel, "America is one of the last, first world countries that attaches our healthcare to our jobs." Therefore, we are told that if we don't have a high paying job, we do not deserve adequate healthcare. The wheel of oppression does not stop and won't until everyone opens their eyes and decides to do something about it.

I know I've mentioned it before, but white people, please make sure to watch Ava DuVernay's "13th" Documentary. In it, she speaks on the reinvention of oppression. With each outlawed form, a new one is created to continue the cycle, and the school system is no different. I experienced the difference in school systems first hand while growing up in Indianapolis. IPS is the largest school district in the city and covers a lot of the inner city and typically lower income areas. On the contrary, you have the township and suburbs of Indy that are better funded, and have more academic achievements. You can guess for yourself which group makes up majority of each.

Moving around a lot as a kid, I attended several different schools and as a student, you can feel the difference in the quality of each experience. I attended private schools, Catholic schools, and several public schools. Now in my professional life, I have had the opportunity to serve children from different backgrounds. I've worked with white students in one of the most affluent cities in the country, Carmel,

Indiana. In my work, I was paid to teach very small children the basics in sports. The organization has so much money that we were able to provide kids with the finest facilities and opportunities. I've also worked at summer camps in black neighborhoods where we were just trying to give the kids constructive things to do in the summer with little to no resources. I currently work in a predominantly Hispanic community, in a school that is passionate about giving the students every opportunity to succeed in a world that tells them they're nothing more than physical laborers. I've seen the world of education through many different eyes and I will tell you that the differences are as vast as you can imagine. I'm done settling for less because I was born black. I will never allow any student to settle for less because of the same reason. If you don't care about the children, I don't care about you. It doesn't matter if you are white, black or brown.

Ideas

1. The key is ensuring the students are motivated. Allow them and their parents to choose what they want to learn from the very beginning. You obviously still incorporate reading, writing, and mathematics into their curriculum but a lot of their time could be spent learning what they want and at their own pace. This way, if a student knows what they want to do their whole life, they can be well on their way by the time they are 18. Then they can either continue building their career which they might already have started, or choose to go to college. Less student debt would be accumulated, and students may be able to become financially independent before enduring four years of college. This should help level the playing field and keep kids in

school who would otherwise drop out. Also, teach kids about their history. Not just white history.

2. I also had the opportunity to interview Cordaryl, also known as "C-Money", who is another member of my close friend circle. Money is a straight shooter that will never let anyone speak ill of you. He now spends his time as a recruiter and finds pride in helping people find employment. Money says, "black history is what keeps me motivated." He knows the great things that his ancestors have accomplished throughout history because he sought out that information as an adult. He admires his father who has been there with him every step of the way. See, if we empower minority students to feel proud of where they come from, you all will be able to better understand why we are so hungry to succeed. You'll learn that not all of us come from a lineage of underachievers but we also have examples of people who do amazing things. Right now, you just lead us to believe that we are criminals who are less than everyone else.

IV.

Red, White, and Blue

"Cops give a damn about a negro
Pull the trigger, kill a nigga, he's a hero
Give crack to the kids, who the hell cares?
One less hungry mouth on the welfare!"
First ship em dope and let em deal to brothers
Give em guns, step back and watch em kill each other
It's time to fight back, that's what Huey said
Two shots in the dark, now Huey's dead."

-Tupac (Changes)

I'm sure you all understand that gangs exist and for whatever reason, people continue to join gangs across the country every day. We've all had the terms "crips" and "bloods" beaten into our heads for decades like they're the only gangs that exist. We know how the media operates though so that makes sense. Members of these gangs are almost portrayed as inhumane mindless animals and it just so happens that gangs are always portrayed as a minority issue. You would think that a country that is so powerful and wealthy would look at these situations and really try to understand why it continues to plague our cities. Instead, America has turned its back on them and criminalized anyone whose skin color has a hint of brown.

You must understand that black people are not the only people in this world who form gangs. Yet, we are the poster children of gun violence and drugs. Our image has been ripped apart by people who don't even know us. Have you ever stopped to think how this came about? You can't possibly believe that we are genetically made to be violent and drug abusers. We live in a country that has withheld all power from us since we were captured and brought over in the slave ships. Therefore, crack had to be placed in our communities. Poor people in these neighborhoods didn't go searching for crack. Crack cocaine found us. Though it caused major damage to our communities, some of our brightest minds focused on how to leverage the crack epidemic to feed their families. Drug dealing is not solely a minority occupation. Many white men deal prescription drugs that do far more damage. You all simply outlawed our way of doing it and represented your approach as if the drugs you sell are necessary to the world. Even in our struggle, we show our magic and that is what I believe you have always been afraid of. Gangs neither start, nor end with black people, so please stop assuming that this is unique to our communities well in fact, the real rival gang was not formed by black people at all. It was formed to represent our opposition.

You must know that most people do not join gangs because they want to wreak havoc on their neighborhoods with violence and drugs. These kids are no different from yours, but the environment and systems you've put in place leaves them with few options. Broken homes lead to a lot of idle time for children. With many amazing moms working crazy hours, children tend to lack the supervision that comes with a parent being in the home. The streets provide a brotherhood for kids who have no one else to turn to. They also provide protection for those same kids, which is essential in some situations. Either way, these are children whom the government refuse to invest in. No human grows up wanting to be violent and harm others. I know for a fact that my black brothers and sisters are no exception. No matter where you grow up, you are a product of your environment. If your environment is filled with stable homes, pool boys, neighborhood associations and country clubs, that's all you see so you view it as the norm. If your environment consists of poverty, drugs and police brutality, you become desensitized to that as well. If any other group of people was placed in these gang-infested neighborhoods, I believe we would have the same results and face the same issues. In these same neighborhoods, grow creators and influencers like Kendrick Lamar, Michael Eric Dyson and Chris Gardner among countless others. We can succeed while battling all odds. We have no other choice because so many obstacles have been placed in front of us and we are trained to fight through them. Gangs just come with the environment. Unless you're the gang with red and blue flashing lights.

I need my white friends to open your mind and try to understand black people's relationship with the police. I just want you to hear me out for just a second. I appreciate every officer who goes into work every morning with the intent of keeping us all safe. It takes a very brave individual to protect strangers every day. You all have families that depend on you and deserve to see you come home. I have met some amazing police officers in my lifetime who represent their departments in the best possible light. What I do not have respect for is The System that breeds the officers. You feel safe when you see their cars, while we tend to feel fear. This institution was created with deep discrimination towards people who look like me. The institution that allows its own members to kill black people at disproportionate rates and let them go home to their families afterward. The institution that allows its officers to search through a woman's privates on the side of the road. Some of these people deserve to be in prison for a very long time. They should take the cell inhabited by a low time marijuana dealer. Instead, they rarely lose their jobs. You may have grown up in a neighborhood that viewed members of law enforcement as upstanding members of the community. I am not here to tell you any differently. Those officers probably live in those neighborhoods and know the opinions of the people in those neighborhoods. You have officers that are comfortable with you and know you outside their uniform. They know what you want and need. They understand the people in those neighborhoods. I'm here to tell you, things sometimes go a little differently on the other side of town.

When officers are targeting us, it rips our families apart. Whether a black person is shot and killed by police or thrown in jail for years, their children may suffer the most. When you eliminate someone as influential as a child's parent out of their life, those are less positive images that they directly see every day. Which can ultimately limit the child to only pursue the things in his or her life that they see. My cousin, Wes who also doubles as my best friend is a testament to what can be achieved when you have influencers who have accomplished a lot raising them. My

Aunt Vanessa is a college graduate and continues to rise up the ranks in her career. "My mother always brought up college, so that's what I wanted to do." She put an impression on him that college was just another part of life. When you lock a child's parent away, like the criminal justice system does every day to black people, that's one less person in a child's life who could leave a positive impression on them. Wes also had a black male teacher throughout school that served as his mentor. Mr. Dobbs encouraged Wes everyday via his mentoring group, Young Men of Purpose. Aunt Vanessa and Mr. Dobbs were able to make a way for themselves and in return guide younger people to do the same. When the police come into our neighborhoods and take people away at alarming rates, kids see that and typically aren't as lucky as Wes. As an award, winning high school teacher, he understands that privilege by explaining during our interview, "Representation is a big deal!" He now dedicates his life to do the same for the students walking the halls of his school.

On the east side of Indianapolis, where poverty is just as common as sidewalks, some police officers take on the role of authoritarian, or overseer, if you will. These officers do not live in these communities. Rarely do they take time to get to know the people in these communities and at most, don't care to. When you only see someone's actions in a troubled situation and have no clue to the reasoning of those actions, misunderstandings can occur. Over time, those misunderstandings turn into prejudices, discrimination and eventually oppression. Then, law enforcement doesn't look at us as neighbors or equals but people they have to keep in check. They only see us fighting to survive in a community that wasn't built for us to do that in the first place.

Tension grows thicker every day and a lot of times that tension bursts, like in the murder of Michael Brown in Missouri. First off, I want to send my utmost respect to

Michael's family, friends and community. Though I do not fully understand your pain, I feel the raw emotion and Michael's life also inspired me to write this book. Now I am sure that some of may be thinking, well he was breaking the law. Without all the facts, I can't determine that. Though laws were made to keep us oppressed to begin with, so when we break some of them, the consequences don't fit the crime. None of us were given a say in the laws, instead laws were created by people who don't even know us. They were created to benefit you and keep me oppressed.

Ferguson, MO is a predominantly black city. So, this fits the mold of officers patrolling people that they possibly have never had any positive interaction with. That's the first strike. I'll respect you more as an officer if you truly understand why I do what I do. Also, we, as black people have been raised to understand that one must be very careful when dealing with the police. Most times we see them in our neighborhood, it's not a friendly interaction. They don't come on the block to have fun and play with kids in our neighborhoods. For the most part, they come to force their will onto already oppressed people, who are trying to make it out of their situation. What really enrages me is that we see police safely apprehend armed white suspects all the time. We know that they have been trained to do so and it has worked for so long. Only thing is, their techniques seem to be different when dealing with black people. We don't even have to be armed to be killed by a police officer, yet we see armed white men be granted the benefit of the doubt and escorted to police stations unharmed. You know that's wrong, yet most of you do nothing about it. When we protest afterwards, you send in armed swat teams to keep us in control. When racists march holding torches on a college campus, they are just exercising their free speech. No cop in sight and it is very possible that they were the ones marching in the first place. Lastly, because of what I mentioned earlier in this chapter, law enforcement automatically sees us as a threat, with, or without weapons. I'm seen as a threat to some people by simply putting my hood up on my head even when it's cold outside. So, in Michael Brown's case, law enforcement is willing to shoot first and ask questions later. The tension among us and police departments are now so thick that I genuinely fear for my life when I see a police car. I double check to make sure I am doing everything right because the slightest missteps can cost me my life.

So, what makes a group of people a gang? Colors that represent them, like red and blue? Gun violence, like killing people and not going to jail? Drug trafficking for profit, like when raids occur and only a certain amount of the recovered drugs are turned over to authorities? The relationship among black people and the police look very similar to the relationship among rival gangs. The reason a lot of drug kingpins thrive is that they have police on the payroll to do some of their dirty work "legally." It's not so hard to believe that a police officer making 50 thousand dollars a year will get his hands a little dirty if they can double their income. Police frequently raid and take these "criminals" possessions without even arresting them at times. These officers I speak of are simply competition to the gang and street leaders in these communities. A lot of them aren't looking to protect the people in the communities but take what they have while punishing them in the process. They could take an hour to respond to your house getting broken into but will be the first on the scene when they know they can make some money.

Across the country, police departments are made up of some of the bravest people on earth. People who live their lives protecting others from danger. I'd like to believe that these brave men and women do not fall into the category that I have explained but it is time to call a spade a spade. We've seen too many tragedies in this country for us not to examine police corruption and brutality. It shows that we are content with the way black people are treated by the police. The country doesn't stand up to white supremacists until they start using terms like neo-Nazi. It goes to show just how much our government truly cares about people who live in anything less than a neighborhood with roundabouts and cul de sacs.

The police pull us over at a higher rate than you. We are arrested at a higher rate than you, and we are sent to prison with longer sentences than you. I don't think this could be clearer. There are police officers who sit quietly and congratulate fellow officers for using abusive force when dealing with minorities. This mindset reaches from the lowest ranking officer to the police chief. This makes officers who do have values and morals afraid to speak up because they don't want to be blackballed or worse, lose their job.

Police officers must stop coming into our neighborhoods and questioning us about our every move. Don't assume that because I'm in a predominantly black area, I'm there partaking in criminal activity. I have no type of criminal record whatsoever, but when police speak to me, they speak down to me. They try to dig up something to arrest me for. I know for a fact that they don't speak to your sons that way. Instead, their tone is calmer, and they look for reasons to let the kid go rather than send him to jail. Don't tell me that I need to respect the police to the highest degree when they don't even respect my life. I was raised correctly, but I will not keep accepting any type of aggression towards me, including from authorities like the police. Don't yell blue lives matter when you criticize us for shouting Black Lives Matter when you gun us down for no reason. You're so sensitive and fragile that you can't handle us sticking up for ourselves. You fear that we would treat you all the same way you treat us. You know how oppressed we are. You are not naive, you know we are treated like the scum of the earth. So, if you have a heart, why don't you do something about it instead of attacking us when we try to change our situation.

My intention this entire time has been for you to see the country that we live in through our eyes. Look, police are necessary in America, but stop holding them on this pedestal like they are gods. They were put in place to enforce a system meant to keep me and other black people in bondage. I'm sick of it. Of course, we all are not the same, just like you all aren't, but if you don't know what we go through, there is no way that you can understand us. All I want is for us to be given fair and equal chances to succeed because we deserve it. If you refuse to give us our rights, don't be surprised when some of us decide to take them ourselves. For those who still find it hard to imagine a police officer being rude and disrespectful for no reason, I'll share my first major run-in with the police, when they showed no respect for me or what I stand for.

As a senior in high school, I along with four of my friends were driving home after a night of trying to get girls' phone numbers. There wasn't any light on the street, so I turned my bright lights on. As we got closer to home, I forgot to turn them off and then, I see those red and blue lights in my rearview mirror. Now, this was well before the days of cell phone footage capturing white officers shooting and killing black people. So, black people getting shot for no reason wasn't at the front of my mind, even though I'm sure it still happened. Although this wasn't a nationwide topic at that time in 2006, my family always taught me to obey police and use the manners they had instilled in me at an early age because they knew what the alternative was.

Two cops walked up to the car, because somehow there were two squad cars behind me. I ended every sentence with sir, and I spoke the way they wanted me to because my life was on the line. I knew that one small slip could send us all straight to jail, or maybe worse. I answered every question truthfully and confidently. As the officer suspiciously examined my driver's license and the other shone his flashlight through my car, I started to get even more nervous because he had no intention of showing me respect. I remembered that my license still had my grandparent's address on it which is on the other side of town in the hood, so I knew that was going to be a topic of conversation. The officer asked me what we are doing on that side of town, as though young black men, like ourselves weren't allowed to leave the eastside of Indianapolis. I thought, 'I travel these streets every day to get to school, work and eventually home.' I played it cool though and apologized for not yet updating my license, which is not illegal by the way. He proceeded to ask me where I was going and why I was heading that way. I politely explain to him that I'm heading home and because he doesn't believe me, he asked me to give him directions on how to get there. He was assuming that I made my destination up, so he put me through a test. The next questions were so that he could find out if I was familiar with the area. I was then very frustrated because all this was just because I had my high beams on. I continued to end my sentences with sir because I was already too skinny for jail and I had things to do the next day. The officers then walked back to their cars, and we all sat there pissed off. We knew that the officer had called for another car before I even pulled over because he saw four black boys in a car at 12:30 a.m. with hoods and baseball caps on. Luckily, this was before I was a race car driver so my driving record was clean and I had all my papers, so I wasn't too worried.

The officers came back, still shining their flashlights all in the car and he asked me to get out of the car. Obviously, I thought for what? But I knew it was in my best interest not to ask, so I complied. He then shone his light around my seat and my friends in the car. This was before I knew my rights, so I just waited until he was done because I knew there was nothing illegal in the car. The officer then turned to me, told me to get back in, and in his most authoritative tone, he asked, "Boy can you read?" I really wanted to smack him in his face at this point. He did nothing but disrespect me for no reason. Last time I checked, he was neither my mother nor father, so him calling me boy was a sign of him feeling superior. In my head, I'm thinking about how I've treated him with nothing but respect, but since I'm in a car with high beams on, I don't deserve the same from him. Driving while black is a serious offense that could at times result in the death penalty, so I decided to maintain my control. Also, no one in my life had ever asked me if I could read, especially someone who feeds their family with my tax dollars. But again, I said, "yes sir I can read." He then threw my registration papers onto my lap and asked me to read it to him. At that point, I was humiliated because where I'm from, this is yet another sign of disrespect. You don't throw anything at anyone, not even money. I read it aloud, and it instructed me to sign my registration, which I had not done. I didn't think of anything that I had done to that point deserving of the response he gave me. I signed it, he handed me my ticket and told me to get out of there.

Luckily I had parents and relatives who taught me to respect police officers no matter what because; our families could have been planning funeral arrangements and he would have gotten a paid vacation. The problem is though, you can give an officer all the respect they deserve, but it can still lead to you losing your life. It's like we're held to higher standards than the people sworn in to protect and serve us. Though on this day, these lessons of respect and following orders saved my life that day and my parents knew that they would. They knew what that police officer was going to think of my friends and I. That officer had no respect for me and assumed the worst before I even pulled the car over. I remember being traumatized by this occurrence and although all my encounters with police have not been this extreme, I know that some are not here to protect me but automatically see me as the enemy because of the color of my skin.

Now, to my white readers, I want you to think back on a time when you had an encounter with police, and they felt like you didn't belong where ever you were. Have they ever insulted you by asking can you read, when they could clearly see that you were old enough to buy cigarettes and go to war for this country they love so much? The point of my text is not to expand on issues the black community seems to have with the police, but I am here to let America know that I do not feel protected by them, whether they are white or black. The judicial system is not set up to protect me but to throw me in prison and disrupt families and future families in the black community. I am grateful to be in America and enjoy some of the privileges we have in this country, but the gratefulness can only go so far when you know red and blue lights in your rearview mirror can mean your last few moments on this earth.

Ideas

1. First, require police to live within a certain radius of the neighborhoods they patrol. Also, streamline the communication among the kids and the police in the neighborhood. Use social media for kids to voice their opinions to law enforcement. Allow kids to visit the local police stations so that they can realize that it's not a place where they would want to wind up. Feed them pizza and let them play video games for an hour on Tuesdays. This is a way for the kids to express to the police what they want and the police to take their feelings into consideration. Kids and the local police station

will all grow to be more comfortable with one another and builds useful bonds.

2. Require the police to go through racial tension training. I know this has been said time and time again, but until it truly happens, we won't know the possible effect it can have.

3. Hold officers to a higher standard. They have some of the most difficult and dangerous jobs anyone can have, but if they are abusing their power, their role is does more harm than good. If a cop takes the life of an innocent person, suspend them without pay. If it is shown that they have used excessive force, take their badges away and they need to be brought up and convicted of a crime. Unfortunately, this seems like a lot to ask. It's a shame that asking for someone to pay the consequences for taking a black person's life is asking too much.

4. Address the harmful relationships within the police force. Create an anonymous system where officers can report other officers who are abusing their power. A lot of good officers are silenced with the fear of being blackballed.

V.

No, You Can't Call Me Nigga

"So what are you supposed to do? My friends, what I need you to do—just for starters—is not act. Not yet. Not first. First I need you to see. I need you to see the pains and possibilities of black life, its virtues and vices, its strengths and weaknesses, its yeses and nos. I need you to see how the cantankerous varieties of black identity have been distorted by seeing black folk collectively as the nigger. It is not a question of simply not saying nigger; you have to stop believing, no matter what, that black folk are niggers and all the term represents. Instead you must swim in the vast ocean of blackness and then realize you have been buoyed all along on its sustaining views of democracy."

— Michael Eric Dyson, Tears We Cannot Stop: A Sermon to White America

I really can't think of a more polarizing word in the English language. This word has evolved so many times and has taken on so many meanings. This one word can mean so many things for so many people. I'm not here to tell you anything that you have not already heard. The argument based around this word has been going on ever since we were brought over here on slave ships. If I can accomplish one thing in this chapter, I would hope it's that you leave with a better understanding of my view on the word. Also, I want you to understand that black people are intelligent and creative in our own right. None of us are the same so therefore, we do not all think alike nor share the same opinions on topics. I can say though that our experiences are similar and we all know that we walk through life in this country and deal with people who do not look like us every day.

By this time, you know what word I am referring to, so I'll refrain from saying it for reasons that I'll explain shortly. First, I would like to address my beautiful black people that use this word as often as I do. I grew up hearing the word at home, in the streets, in movies and music just like you did. It has been engrained into my brain whether I wanted it a part of my vocabulary or not. I know how we use it and also how it was used against us. I understand the origin of it just like you do and I also how we magically flipped it in attempt to suppress the feelings of oppression that it originally represented.

Black people, I mean it with love when I say, it wouldn't hurt for us to slow down the use of this word. Now, I know this may be an unpopular opinion amongst the millennial generation but hear me out first, before you close this book and say, "he doesn't know what he is talking about." I'm no hypocrite, I use the word just as much as the next black person, if not more. I've been saying it since I can remember and have not felt wrong in doing so. I'm an advocate for Hip Hop music where it at times is used on every line. With all these being said, I do try to be more conscious of how often I say it. I feel like it's a word that we can keep in-house. One can remember their mom telling them as children, "Don't tell my business" or "What happens here, stays here"? This is the approach I feel like we should take. I personally do not say the word in front of white people. In my opinion, it makes them feel comfortable enough to say it as well. I also do not use it when referring to a white people because it simply doesn't feel right. We don't need to let them in on everything we do. It's okay to keep some aspects of our culture among us.

To spare you the confusion, I think we should just keep it in "mama's house." We all know you use it amongst yourselves and there's nothing that we can do about that. I personally just take it as a compliment because once again, it shows that our charisma and the way we carry ourselves is admired by all. Appropriating African American culture is now the norm because we make a lot of things cool. I don't want to continue the topic without addressing my brothers and sisters who allow white people use it in their presence. First off, when I hear it come out of your mouths, I cringe. All I hear is generational hatred and oppression come out of your mouths, and I personally cannot stand for it. We are feeding your sense of superiority whether we mean to or not. You may feel like they are using it as a term of endearment but wait until you make them mad or you get out of their sight, the tone behind the word can change very quickly. Also, if they say it around you, they may try their chances of saying it around someone else which is setting them up for failure. Don't say it's not a big deal because it most certainly is. A white person with any level of morality won't want to utter that word anyway. When you allow them to say it, it encourages the argument of slavery and oppression are things of the past. Therefore, they live their lives believing discrimination doesn't exist. Racism is just as alive today as it was during slavery. You can argue that it is even more profound today with it being so deeply rooted and disguised. Look at it like this; the word is a curse word that only black people use amongst one another. You don't go into a meeting with colleagues and rattle off curse words. If you do, and its acceptable, that is one thing, but I'd say most employers don't allow that. If you must, feel free to use it amongst your people, but try to keep it that way. Also, if we allow this word to be used in our presence by white people, it can very likely transition to conversations of outspoken superiority on the part of white people. I am not suggesting that this will certainly happen, but why even take that risk? We have to demand their respect because waiting it will only slip us farther and farther behind the more we wait. You don't have to live your entire life walking the line of white fragility. We are not here to lose apart of ourselves to make them feel comfortable, because the same has never been reciprocated.

Most of us will never be famous artists, who are the only people who can get away with using the word in the presence of white people in my opinion. Art is art and when you put a limit on it, that's when you deprive yourself of enjoying great masterpieces. So please remember, I'm not trying to change you, I just want to open a door of thought that may have been closed in your mind. I'm here to just start the conversation, and I want to hear how you feel about this as well. Just think about it. Know that I love you, black people and we can vote on this at the next BBQ.

White people, I think you should know that I still believe some of you are actually good people. Unfortunately, I don't know if it's as many of you as you may think. I'm not one of those people that say all of you are racist. I just think at least half of you are. The ones that may not be racist, but thrive on their privileges without acknowledging the oppression that their people put us under are just as bad as the racists. Now I just want to be honest. I think the only way we can actually get to know one another is if we keep it real. I mentioned in the previous chapter that I welcome all comments on my thoughts throughout these pages.

First off, you all don't know us, so don't try to act like it, unless you are actually taking steps to learn. You all don't even know half of us. You have absolutely no idea how it feels to be black. Just the same as I have no idea what it's like to be white, but with me being engulfed in your everyday lives, I do have a clue. Since the very day that you were born, this world has been placed you in power and keeps all the rest of us down in the basement somewhere. You strip us of every single aspect of our culture that we allow you to see. You attempt to make it your own but can never figure it out well enough to make it feel real. Every single thing in this country was made for you and to benefit you. Your privilege runs generations deep, and there is no denying it.

My people are so magical that we were able to come out of years of literal bondage and turn a word that was used in a derogatory fashion into one that can be used in several scenarios within the black community. When you think, you have us down, we twist out of your oppression and flip it in a way that you're constantly reminded of how perseverant we are. You pull a lot of things from our culture, but that word is one I will not stand to see you try your hands at. I truly believe you all would understand it if you would just think about it. This word was used when your ancestors were violating black women. It was used to execute us in more ways than I'd like to count. We don't take disrespect from one another so there is absolutely no way you will get away with disrespecting any of us. We're a different breed; we work too hard for what we have in this country to be disrespected by someone who doesn't even know our struggle. We climbed hills taller than you've ever seen to make it where we are.

You think I should accept you saying this word in my presence? My skin crawls when the first sound of the word seeps out of your lips. You don't know me, nor what I go through, so I will not allow you to have that oppressive exchange of dialogue.

Why do you want to say it so badly? What about it is so enticing to you that you refuse to refrain from the word. I understand that we make a lot of things cool, but we have given you a lot of material already, so use those. I know you'll say it behind closed doors and there's nothing I can do about that. I just ask that you respect me, and everything I represent by not spewing the words of your misguided ancestors. You are also more than welcome to come up with a term of endearment that is less offensive to me. You can create one for yourselves so that you don't have to depend on us and our creativity. Other groups of people tend to be respected more than black people are. I am not saying that other races don't deserve it but why does it seem like we don't. What did we do to you all that hurt you so badly? We didn't come to your home land and drag you off to a foreign place. We didn't force you to work on plantations. We didn't rape your women and rip your families apart. How long do you think we will endure the disrespect that is directed at us every day? Just let us have what we have, you all have enough. When you say the word, it comes along with key ingredients. One cup of slavery, a dash of death and rape. It brings with it a bucket of oppression and heavily sprinkled hatred. It's then baked in an oven of Jim Crow, incarceration and poverty. So, you must know that you are upsettingly wrong when you say it's just a word. It's a dish that has been making my people sick for centuries. If it's just a word, then don't say it.

If you feel attacked, please don't. It is my intent for you to feel my emotion in each line. I'm tired. The cycle of oppression is getting old and the older I get, the less patience

I have for it. I really do think that we can live in a society that's comfortable for all of us. Do I have hope like Obama says he does? I'll be the first to say the hope I had has been drained like a gas leak. That doesn't mean that I don't think it is possible. I want you all to understand how serious I am because it means that much to me. I am living among you, and I go to work and serve kids who will one day lead our country in a way that's beneficial to everyone.

Like I've stated numerous times already, this book is intended to get that conversation started. Like I tell the students I work with, if we really knew one another, we wouldn't treat one another so badly. If you knew us, you would know that we aren't trying to control any type of people. I don't think we feel the need to keep other races oppressed so that we can dominate. We can achieve great things without stepping on other's heads to get there. We just want to live our lives, raise our beautiful children in a world that provides them with just the same opportunities as everyone else. Right now, that couldn't be any farther from the case. Just leave the word alone, or make up your own word. You have already taken so much from us, so don't compound it by disrespecting us, because you know we don't take disrespect well.

Ideas

1. Educate kids in school on the actual root of the word and how it was used. Both black and white children. This way, black people can make a choice for themselves whether to use it or not based on what they've learned. I hope you will learn that it is, in fact, more than just a word.
2. Put new employees through racial sensitivity training when they get new jobs. Make it as serious as sexual assault in the workplace.

People, for the most part, take their jobs seriously and wouldn't want to do anything that would jeopardize it.

3. Lastly, don't allow your older relatives to say it in front of the children. Treat it like a curse word. If white kids aren't exposed to the word they will be less likely to use it. You probably won't have success trying to persuade adults to refrain from using it. Just like a lot of other approached in this book, it is not too late to mold the younger generation.

VI.

The System

"Every day we fight the system just to make our way
We been down for too long, but that's alright
We was built to be strong, cause it's our life, na-na-na
Every day we fight the system, we fight the system
We fight the system (Never like the system)
We been down for too long but that's alright, na-na-na"

-Kendrick Lamar ft. Alori Joh (Hiiipower)

You all have been able to accomplish a great feat. What you have created here in America is a sociological experiment that has gone exactly how you all planned it to go. I think one of the most amazing things about it is, most of you do not even realize it exists. It's something that was created by you and for you. It's been hidden from you so that the pure image of the white race remains intact. If you actually knew what your people have done, anyone with a conscious would understand that this country is not all it says it is. If you really open your eyes, you'd be amazed at what you all have been able to accomplish. Your ancestors have put so many things in place to maintain the power you have over everyone else in this country all while maintaining a glistening reputation. Well, in your eyes at least.

The System, as I will refer to it here, was built with hate and selfishness. It's made up of laws, traditions, and biases that have been used as building blocks to create the massive building of oppression. It has endured years of societal progression. It has survived decades of great African American Civil Rights Leaders who speak out against it. The System has outlasted every protest, sit in and riot. It's what keeps us hopeless as a collective minority. The System was built a long time ago for no one but you. This Chapter, like the rest, is not meant to badger you but to inform you of the truth as the minorities know it, and as you should too.

Since we were young school kids, we were taught to admire the brave Christopher Columbus who traveled far across the water in search of new land. We all know that resulted in Native Americans being slaughtered throughout this land and Columbus got a holiday named in his honor. Now, there is no way that you all would allow someone to come over here today and take America away from us. What made this situation ok in Columbus' opinion was that the Native people were not as civilized. Though this does make me think, who said you all are the perfect example of a civil human being? Anyway, we were taught to praise Columbus for his heroic work. American history was written by old white men who were looking to portray their people in the best light possible, but we all know that our history books leave out very important aspects of our history. This is a crucial part of The System because if you don't know what happened in the past, you can't explain the present or future. If you don't know that you stole land and free labor to start this country, you are overwhelmingly naïve. This history is not just taught to you but minorities as well. It's very easy for minorities to start to believe some of the rhetoric we are fed. Constant negative rhetoric can weaken one's pride in whom they are and where they come from. We go through school learning the same thing you all do, except we go home to live and see a different truth every day. America continues to portray Christopher Columbus as a moral and brave man. You all tend to think so highly of yourselves that you don't see the injustice that is right in front of you on cell phone footage.

As we matriculate through the American education system, we find more and more examples of skewed history that is used to deceive our perspective of reality. Thomas Jefferson is considered one of the greatest US President of all time. Thomas Jefferson not only owned a slew of slaves but raped and used black women as sex dolls. He abused them with no remorse. Black women are queens and for him to do those filthy things makes me cringe. All respect to the great advancements he made for this country, but I have no respect for him or his legacy. Black women get treated so badly, but white men can't seem to keep their hands off of them. They experience discrimination based on their sex and race but are arguably the most intelligent and strongest group of people this planet has ever seen. They can overcome anything you put in front of them. Even the dirty, scum of the earth rapists who want nothing from them but their perfectly crafted bodies. Yet, as a child, we were taught to respect and appreciate all he did for our country but never are we taught about his sick fantasies which he carried out with his helpless black slaves.

Obviously, I have to mention the brief chapters on slavery that barely get any attention. Slavery is minimized in history books intentionally. This country was built on the backs of slaves, and for some reason, we often found the time to highlight the "good" slave masters who didn't beat their slaves as much as other masters. When you take a group of people away from their homeland, bring them to a foreign place shackled in the belly of inhumane conditioned slave ships and force them to work for roughly 200 years, I think that deserves more than just a chapter in a history book. My people were stripped of their culture, language, religion and everything they knew. Our families were torn apart, and we were left to sleep on dirt beds of despair. You forced their culture on my ancestors because once again, we were considered barbaric and needed the white man to save us. The plot twist though is that now our culture is one of the most replicated and admired with little to no recognition. Beyond slavery, any black man or woman who spoke out against the injustices of The System are either not mentioned or portrayed as a violent radical, take Malcolm X for example. There have been plenty of books written on slavery by my black brothers and sisters that take you a little deeper, but I want you to know that the act of bias history reporting is the foundation of The System.

It doesn't stop at distorting history to paint white people in the most positive light. Something that lasts beyond our high school history class is the media, which we now consume at rates similar to the speed of light. The media, which is owned by rich white men that sit on the board of directors of Fortune 50 companies, is just as distorted as our history books. Your leader of this nation loves to mention fake news but says nothing when black people are unfairly portrayed as criminals and thugs. The media is the easiest way to warp the minds of as many people as possible. That's why when a black man is killed by the police, it is represented totally different from when a white woman is killed by the police under the same condition.

When Justine Damond tragically lost her life at the hands of police, a picture was shown of her in full makeup, smiling, in front of tropical palm tree leaves. It honestly looked like her LinkedIn profile or the picture on the back of her autobiography. When she died, the focus was shifted to the officer being a Muslim who killed a completely innocent white woman. Philando Castile was murdered by the police, and the media pushed the darkest and meanest pictures of him they could find. Instead of explaining why the officer was wrong, they focused on arguing why the officer acted in the right manner. There is no one checking to make sure news outlets are clear of bias. They paint pictures how they want, and you must know that they won't be reporting anything that goes against people who look like the owners.

This is the same System that incarcerates black people at alarming rates. The criminalist identity that is applied to black people is not by mistake. After slavery and sharecropping, the wheel was reinvented as mass incarceration. When you teach the school children that black people are violent criminals, and you make sure to keep positive images of black people off the television screen and media, you mold the minds of citizens into believing that black people belong in prison. That is how the justice system can arrest black people much more frequently and give them longer sentences than white men who commit the same crime. When you make the drugs most frequently used by black people appear to be the worst drugs available, you can lock us up more. If you can link that same drug to a life of criminal activity, even better.

The easy comparison is crack vs. cocaine. The sentences for crack are much longer than the sentences for cocaine because you all tend to use cocaine and black people tend to choose the less expensive version, crack. Take this into account; weed has been deemed one drug that is plaguing our society. At one point, it seemed to be the most talked about and therefore considered the most lethal. In reality, it kills less people than both forms of cocaine and heroin, which are typically used by you. While growing up, if you get caught with any weed, you are going straight to jail. You can imagine how that translates to black men being over-represented in our prisons. Now it's becoming more and more legal by the year, and you have caught on to the financial gain that comes with it. The idea of selling weed has gone from being for black criminals to white men making millions of dollars off legal weed because they have the resources to open the dispensaries. Yet, all black men and women are still in prison for the same drug that is making white men rich. This is The System at its peak. It allows black men to go to jail for doing the same thing white men make millions of dollars while doing.

It seems as though The System is rooted deeper than even I can even imagine because as I grow and educate myself, I naturally make more and more connections to The System. I find new building blocks everywhere I go. In our society, it's all about finding a job. Not creating anything but gaining the tools to help someone else bring their ideas to life. The people we are helping are the people who had access to the resources to make their vision come to life, or the role models to show them that it was possible. I'm speaking of you, white people. We are taught to get an education that you crafted to get a job that you provide. Therefore, attempting to make us dependent on you. The necessary resources like the knowledge or funding to create something of your own have typically been withheld from us and kept in country clubs and cul-de-sacs. You tell us how to act when we come in to meet you which is vastly different from how we comfortably live in our homes. You tell us that we can't shake hands the way we are accustom to because it's not professional. You tell us how we need to communicate because we make you uncomfortable when we speak the way we do to one another, or you simply don't understand what we may be saying. Therefore, you can let us go or refuse us the job because we don't fit the 'culture.' I personally feel like I can accomplish just as much while using slang amongst my colleagues. I am not allowed to though because I have to keep you all comfortable or else I could find myself unemployed. Even in the rare case of solely working with black people, you all have set this precedent where even we still manage to subconsciously uphold your norms even when you aren't around.

The System is made up of many different building blocks that are all dedicated to ensuring you stay in power. Nothing holds as much power as knowledge. I'm speaking of knowledge in every sense of the word. Not only knowledge that is spewed by professors on college campuses, even though we don't experience much of that either. Specifically, I'm speaking of financial knowledge. The knowledge that we can use to pull ourselves out of the projects. While interviewing my good friend Cordaryl, he mentioned to me that creating generational wealth is a key for himself. He realizes that generational wealth is what differentiates a lot of white families from minority families in America. Cordaryl's parents had him as teenagers and didn't have much financial literacy to pass on to him and his siblings. With knowledge of financial do's and don'ts we would be better equipped to provide our families with more opportunities. Now yes, we do have many great examples of financial freedom in the black community, but a lot of those same people did not learn the key factors to wealth until late into adulthood. Most times they did not learn from their parents while growing up. Stocks and assets are not words that we hear a lot of as children. The side of money we see is striving for paychecks, not giving them out. If you have an entire generation that doesn't truly know how to use their money, the next generation is going to be in the same situation, and the cycle of poverty continues. We don't learn how to navigate a corporate ladder. You may say well, neither do we, but the difference is, you don't have to. Your fathers and mothers tend to pull you up the ladder themselves whether you know it or not.

As African Americans, we simply do not have enough power to bring The System down alone. We can work on different aspects of it, but we need your help to eliminate it as a whole. It takes more than you saying there's a problem and then spending the rest of your day basking in your privilege. Even with your privilege, we aren't living to our full potential as a country. We as black people have so much to offer, but right now no one wants to accept it. We can change your life if you let us. The System holds us back in the long run. If we don't take care of it now, it will take care of us. The time to fight systemic racism is now. Just imagine if your child was born to be discriminated against. Our country is built on Christian principles, but The System shows the opposite. God says love thy neighbor as thyself, and I don't feel the love at all. Don't use the Bible solely when it's convenient for your bigotry. Use it to uplift yourself and others. If you don't know what you can do, you can at least start by reaching out to your local leaders and voicing how you feel. Your voice is so much more valuable than you give it credit for, so use it.

Ideas

1. The system needs a total overturn. I don't think this answer can be simplified to a few sentences. The key is addressing each brick of

The System separately. That is what the other chapters in this book are attempting to do.

2. Put a board in place whose job is to go through every new piece of legislation and make sure that it will represent all people equally. This board should be made up of local leaders in the community from every neighborhood who truly represents the people of that area. This could be pastors, school leaders, small business owners, community center leaders, etc. Offer an incentive for the people who sit on the board. Stick to a clear understanding of what this board does and how they operate.

VII.

Black Magic

Black is Beautiful, baby, black is bold
Black is black, true, but black is gold, no, ay, hey, yea, look
I say black is beautiful, shawty, black is bold
Black is black, true, but black is gold

-Wale, "Black is Gold"

It makes sense that some would choose to oppress my people simply because they are intimidated by us. We are some of the most talented people in the world. We can be brilliant academic scholars when given a little opportunity. We are athletes who can compete in any athletic arena that we step into. We are artists who create to transcend generations of people. When I say art, I mean every form of art. Writing, music, painting, dance, acting are all art forms that we have advanced throughout time. Some of the most important inventions were created by my brothers and sisters. Traffic lights, the clothes dryer, and the home security system just to name a few. Think about where you would be without those items. I promise you we have so many more inventions that haven't come to life yet because we don't provide our black children with the tools needed to succeed. Instead of teaching them how to properly conduct themselves in an interview all the time, how about we show them the process of obtaining a patent? Though we are figuratively magic and can achieve feats that have never been achieved before, we are necessary to the progression of the human race in the arenas of science, technology, and medicine.

Without black people, the entire country of the United States would not have come to fruition because black people built this country from the ground up. This is no offense to anyone, but without the amazing contributions of black America, this would be a stale place to reside. It's a shame that we even have to mention how important we are to this country. It should actually be something that is repeatedly recognized and appreciated. Instead, we have to plead for black representation. Your feeling of being threatened should not come from the wise and more boisterous attitude of black people; you should feel threatened by how The System is holding this country back. If African Americans were given the same opportunities as you, who knows what this country can accomplish. We have no interest in belittling you or trying to maintain some type of dominance over your lives. We just want to live and build wealth for ourselves and future generations just like you do. I want to be able to expose my children to the wonders of the world without having to explain to them why we were treated differently than the white family when we walk into a store. You know how intelligent kids are, well I can speak for especially black children. They pick up on every single thing and take notice of the things that go against the morals they've been taught.

Whether you want to believe it or not, black people have provided you with one of the best Presidents your beloved country has ever seen. President Barack Obama led a country full of people who hated him before he even opened his mouth. He led and represented people who would have liked nothing better than to see him hanging from a tree. He led people who truly felt as though he was a second-class citizen.

Meanwhile, he loved and wanted to do right by everyone in this country. Do you know how much poise that requires? To stand up for people who spit in your face and disrespect you and your family? He treated all death threats he received with dignity and an unimaginable calmness. Even though some of you see black people as inferior, the leader of the free country would never even hint at himself being more important than the next citizen. He tried to be a friend to us even though we never met him. He regularly let us know that he was here to represent every American and along with his extraordinary wife, showed that in his actions all eight years. We are talking about the man who led us out of the worst recession since the Great Depression. Even though he accomplished so much, he still faced people hanging a replica of his body from a tree. There were still parades that had floats with monkeys dressed as our Nation's leader. President

Obama has one of the purest hearts, but people still belittled him. That's when I knew that you all could care less about how many accolades someone has because, at the end of the day, we'll always be a nigger.

For a group of people to provide the world with so many magical things, you would think we would just get a ticket when we get pulled over. Instead, we get killed. One would also think that instead of being shot by a neighborhood watch leader, we would hold forums and community discussions on how to get to know one another better. We get choked out for selling single cigarettes. Our children get killed for playing with toy guns. When we do get murdered by The System of injustice, the argument of "well what about black on black crime" is always soon to follow. It's almost like we are the only race that kills one another.

We have to re-evaluate everything from our school systems to our criminal justice systems. Put the same money in our schools that go into the white suburban schools. Give us the same amount of prison time that you give yourselves. Actually, just arrest us at the same rates you do your own people. Give us a fair chance to obtain donations to start our own tech companies, not trying to squeeze us into a corner at your company so you can say your company is diverse. We just want equality. We're not asking to be a part of your lives because you all have implanted enough of your culture into us forcibly. We do want to hang on to what is ours. You all brought us here, now let us live our lives without having to worry about discrimination. It's getting really old, and one day, the tense oppressive systems you have us under will cause us to snap. We really aren't as violent and aggressive as you make us out to be, we haven't even done half as much to you all as you've done to us.

I honestly believe that black people are some of the most intriguing people on this planet. Black people are a precious jewel that should be protected by everyone. We have so much to offer the world with so little resources to do it. That is why we celebrate and support one another that do things that this planet has never seen before because they did it with extra hurdles. I like to think of life as a marathon in the Olympics, in which black people don't come out of the blocks until ten minutes after our opponents. We are expected to "pull ourselves up by our bootstraps" and win the race. They say if we want it bad enough, we'll get it.

To give you an example, there are two people I admire who are quickly growing to be leaders in their industries. I am originally from Naptown, but I moved to the Bay Area about two years ago. Now as you can imagine, these are two very different places in every aspect of the word; obviously starting with the cost of living, weather, population diversity, lifestyle, main industries, mindsets, and everything. I'll say I'm from Nap until the day I die. I love my city, and everyone who knows me knows that I do. I never speak down on anything about the city, but I do support facts. The Bay Area presents much broader opportunities, but it also comes with the mindset that I can do anything I want. Back home, we think very surface level in regards to the potential of our lives. Living here and experiencing so many different types of people and cultures just in this one place, opened my mind. There are two people that help in that transcendence of my mind.

This first individual's simple presence on social media grabbed my attention. Tristan Walker was featured in a Time Magazine early 2016. I saw a young black man with the headline, "Meet the Silicon Valley CEO who is opening doors for People of Color." He has ascended up the ranks in Silicon Valley by using his resources to pull others up with him. I began reading the article, and Tristan talked about how he got his start in the tech industry. Getting directly involved with tech doesn't interest me, but I understand its necessity in our progression as human beings. I was just proud to see him succeed. He proceeded to mention his non-profit organization that works to increase the number of minorities in the world of tech. Code2040 accomplishes this by partnering with tech companies in Silicon Valley and to provide internship opportunities for students in Computer Science. This caught my attention immediately because I was looking for a job at the time and that was exactly the cause I was willing and ready to get behind. Even if coding seems extremely boring to me, Tristan is an example of someone who has feet in both black and white worlds. He carries himself with respect and still respects where he comes from and the people there. He is one of our leaders in the tech industry and wants to bring us all along with him. He'll continue to do amazing things that not only black people, but everyone will benefit from. He deserves to live in a discriminatory free world just like the white colleagues he has come across in his career.

I researched Code2040 and applied for a position in their organization. Later, even though I didn't get the job I applied for, I was hired on part-time basis during their Summer Fellows Program, since I work in education and get summers off. Though I was disappointed, I knew God had other plans for me. I learned that Tristan was actually the co-founder and he had someone who actually ran the organization based out of San Francisco, CA. Upon meeting her, Laura Weidman Powers was just as admirable as she was in her interviews. Her educated yet empathetic demeanor is great for the organization. Powers and her husband are both great people. For those of you that are unfamiliar, Laura graduated cum laude from Harvard College and had a JD and MBA from Stanford. Her work in tech and nonprofits alike has landed her on numerous lists of influential people. Most notably, in 2016, Laura was chosen as a Sr. Advisor to the Chief Technology Officer, Megan Smith by the Obama Administration. She spent six months configuring tactics that our country could use to increase the number of minorities in tech. Laura carries herself in a powerful and professional manner and dedicates her life to providing opportunities for others. She's also one of the realest ones we have because she believes in our abilities to change this world through technology, even when others may not give us a chance.

White people, remember that you will never completely understand us if you sit back in the comfort of your privilege without opening your mind to learn about other groups of people and why they do the things they do. You haven't been in our shoes, and there is no real way to represent our experiences to you. This again, is why I am here. I want you to love and adore the gift God gave the world in the form of black people, or at the very least, respect us. We are resilient people who overcome any barrier placed in front of us, including when at the spades table. We throw amazing cookouts to bring us all together over some of the things we love, like food, alcohol, fellowship, and laughs. We fight for one another for reasons you can never imagine. For the most part, we protect the people we love with everything we have. We all serve a significant role in our communities. We have rhythm because we are typically the ones making all the music. It is later copied and used to entertain many other music lovers around the globe. Good music has been in our lives since way before you all even brought us over here. Sorry, not sorry.

Our family does not only extend to our immediate family members. We love our cousins, aunts, and uncles just as hard because we all need one another. We need one another so that we can make it in this oppressive society which you have created for us. We love one another so much that our family gatherings are always sold out events. When we can finally get around people that look like us and that we love till death, it always sets for a good time. And when you cross us, that's why so many people come out against you. It's just how we are wired. I know for sure that if you cross me, you will hear from someone who I may not have even spoken to in months. I love that about us.

By result, this has made respecting our elders not only a good thing to do, but also mandatory. You all may be hard on us at times, but our own people are harder on us than The System could ever be. So, this is why you don't hear of a black child disrespecting their parent in any way. Word travels fast, so if we were ever to step out of line, our aunts and uncles would know before we are even done crying about it. We could take a wrong path in life but rarely does that mean we do not respect our elders. This is for life, not just as a child. A lot of us saw our mothers raise us by themselves. Sometimes with multiple brothers and sisters. As children, we see how strong our parents are and we see the sacrifices they make for each of us every day. Nothing was handed to me.

There was not much that my mom could do for me, but she did what she had to do, and she provided me with what I needed. We never went long periods of time without at least a roof over our heads at night. I never went without some food to eat, even if it was the fast food poison that The System feeds to poor people. Essentially, when the white girl gets on Dr. Phil and publicly drags her mother through the mud, we can't relate.

Something you also need to know about my people is that we are natural born hustlers. A lot of us come from the bottom, so for people like Oprah, Aliko Dangote, Robert Smith, and P Diddy to make billions in a system that was built against them is overly impressive. They were able to achieve it because they hustle and make sure they get what they want out of life. We may not always be the best at managing our money, probably because we never had it coming up, but we are certainly good at making it. My mom has been hustling to put food on her children's plate for the past 27 years. How many of you think you could have made it happen if you started with less than nothing? Unfortunately, this also means that we have gotten extremely good at making money selling drugs. We obviously are nowhere near the only people who deal drugs, the biggest and richest drug dealers are your dads and uncles who sit atop the drug companies that make billions of dollars a year off prescription drugs. These drugs were placed in our communities by you for strategic reasons. We understand that, but you have criminalized us for doing what we have to do to survive in your country. This country holds me by the neck as I come out of the womb. We saw an opportunity in the 80's when Reagan shipped cocaine to our doorstep. We saw an opportunity to get out of the impoverished communities that had plagued us for generations. One day I want to live in a peaceful neighborhood and go to homeowners' meetings and never have to discuss a crime related problem. We have children too, and we repeatedly try to provide them with the best opportunities. The same thing you want for your children. So, in this scenario, many of us grew to making millions of dollars and employing a lot of people through drug dealing. I am in no sense saying it is the right thing to do because my family would have my head, but you have to admire the quality of making something out of nothing.

Communication is what we need. I am always more than willing to educate white people on the lives that African American lead. I know that at times it can be intimidating for you to start these conversations but you'll feel so much better when you walk away with a better understanding of what we go through. Ask your black neighbors what makes them uncomfortable in your neighborhood? Invite them to your next barbecue and go to theirs. I promise you will always have a good time. Explain to us what you are confused about. Instead of making assumptions, just ask. Keep in mind though, we are not all the same so be prepared to have different interactions with each of us, but the better you communicate, the more you will realize we are not a threat to you. You'll realize that fighting for our equal rights will work to everyone's benefit. I want you to take these conversations that start between these pages, to your friends and family members. Talk to your neighbors and come up with ways you can make your community more inclusive. Teach your kids how to ask to understand rather than assume and appear foolish. Just start talking because that's all I can really ask for.

Ideas

1. Since we have Black History Month, we should actually use it. During the month, instead of black people being the only ones to celebrate, we should highlight past and present influential black people in National media. We should do this for every minority in our country. This way we can try to balance out the negative images of my people that are shown on a daily basis. We are not only criminals. All races have criminals. We are people who look to improve the lives of all people.

2. When it comes to safe spaces where poor kids are able to create, they are few and far between. Maybe we can advocate for some sort of property tax cut for businesses whose mission is providing studios for young people to express themselves. If anything, this could simply be a place to keep kids out of the street. That is what Top Dawg did for Kendrick Lamar and the original members of Top Dawg Entertainment.

VIII.

Protect Them at All Costs

"A project minded individual, criminal tactics
Us black kids born with birth defects, we hyperactive
Mentally sex-crazed, dysfunctional, they describe us
They liars, at the end of the day, we're fuckin survivors"

-Rick Ross ft. Nas (Triple Beam Dreams)

One of the most treasured prizes in the black community is our black children. Birthed from magical black women, comes innocent human beings who are behind before they even start. Being a black child in America comes with great responsibility. You have the hurdle of developing your brain and body while also learning of the oppressed society that you will battle every day for the rest of your life. This is also while you are at times forced to grow up too soon to assist your parents who endure the daily struggles of being a minority in this country. Even before our children know it, they are being judged as violent and incapable human beings. You all are seen as capable adults even when you can barely read. What I mean by that is, when a black child gets into some sort of trouble, they are labeled as young adults, insinuating that they should know better and are fully grown dangerous machines. On the other hand, grown white men will get into some trouble and are labeled as "kids." Just take your "kid," Ryan Lochte for example. When he got into trouble during the Rio Olympics while representing the USA, headlines painted him as a young kid who just made a simple mistake. May I add that he was just cleared to return to competing for the US. Colin Kaepernick took a knee during the anthem to make a statement about the clear police brutality in this country and is still out of a job.

Black Children are treasures. I refuse to see another black child face the outcome that Tamir Rice did. Tamir was 12 years old when he was gunned down by two white male police officers. They took the life of that little boy with no remorse. For those that are shamefully unfamiliar with the incident, Tamir was playing with a toy gun in a Cleveland Park when bystanders called the police when they saw the boy. Instead of finding out if it was a real gun, those witnesses' first step as they saw a black child playing was to call the police. This infers that the police department's sole purpose is to keep people in line. They saw a black child and immediately correlated that with needing police assistance. They called the police who they knew were trained to keep black people in check. They initially referred to Tamir as a man playing with a pistol. Now I'm not sure how often you confuse a 12-year-old boy for a man, but it happened. Like I mentioned before, we are expected to grow up and have the mental capacity far beyond our years. Tamir had barely lived his life before it was taken from him by an organization that only saw the color of his skin. The officer's hot bullets penetrated Tamir's body without even attempting to find out what exactly was going on. All they knew was that a black man was at a park with a gun.

Tamir's chance to battle an oppressive system that wasn't set up for him from the beginning was stripped away before he even entered his teenage years. He didn't get the chance to prove The System wrong by keeping a clean record and making the world a better place for himself and his family. His parents never had the opportunity to see him complete milestones like finishing high school, getting his driver's license, getting a part-time job and finding his first girlfriend. He never had the chance to do any of this because he was black. It's hard to imagine this happening to a white child because it rarely even gets that far. We see police talk white armed men down from committing crimes, but Tamir didn't get that chance.

This enrages me more than a lot of the police brutality killings because we are talking about a precious child. I am an educator. I work in a middle school and deal with 12-year-olds every day. I have the opportunity to see them grow inside and outside the classroom. This is a time when they are going through puberty, and so many changes are occurring in and around them. It's a precious time in a child's life and a prime time in a black child's life when they can choose the trajectory of their life. My students blow me away every day with their many talents and various views of the world. I love the opportunity to help guide them through their adolescence and give them opportunities that I never had. Black children specifically are up against so much and still never cease to amaze me. They battle teachers who don't connect with them. Some battle classmates who know nothing about them but the negative images their families and the media portray. These are times where they realize that they are different from your children and experience life differently. These are resilient children who sometimes go home to no electricity, food or family but still amaze the world with their talents.

I had the pleasure to attend the National Convention for my charter school network in which majority black students had the opportunity to showcase their talents. There were dancers, singers, artists, and writers. My heart was overcome with emotion because my black children are so committed to their craft and are talented far beyond their years. A dance team from Sunnyside, Texas did a routine to the heart-tugging song, "Born by the river" by the great Sam Cooke. These are high school students who have yet to enter the professional world but are already very much familiar with the indecencies in our nation. They use their craft to speak out against everyone who is waiting for them to fail. It was during these performances that the thought of a bigot taking one of their lives away lit a fire in my heart that is still very much alive as I write this book. My black children are not here to terrorize your communities. They are not taught to hate you or your family. When you treat them like second-class citizens, they are intelligent enough to know what is going on and try their best to go about their lives positively. Humans, black, white and everything in between, run off of emotion. When someone is not treated fairly, you have to be ready for however, they choose to react. You can only hold someone down for so long before they decide to do something about it. It's a wonder why more haven't taken the violent route that you all assume we would anyway.

I want you to examine the emotions you feel when you think about your children. You believe your children deserve every opportunity to succeed. You assume your child's innocence until and even after their brain reaches full growth. You believe that their lives are more important than ours as adults. You believe this until the child you are referring to is black.

These black children may have the intellect to create something that could be beneficial not only for themselves but all people. Your disdain for black people is so strong that you would rather eliminate them than see what they can grow to become, which could benefit you in the long run. We will never know if Tamir would live up to the equivalency of Barack or Michelle Obama. Tamir could have been the scientist who discovers the cure for Alzheimer's which currently deteriorates the mind of some of your elders. Tamir could have been the entertainer that you flock to the theaters to see. He could have been the musician that makes music that lives for generations. We will never know this because Tamir was black at the wrong time. All black children are my children, and the instances of them being treated unfairly will not be tolerated. Encourage yourself and family members to withhold their hate and fear for black children- at least until they are old enough to make their own decisions. They are just as precious as your children. I will tell you that another case of Tamir Rice will not be tolerated so for the good of everyone, grant my magical black children the pure innocence that you grant yours.

The term "Black Queen" has never seemed more true to me than it has in the past few years. I am a product of very strong black women myself, and I'm very proud of that fact. Because of that, I hold working hard to provide for myself and my future family very close to my heart. They can do anything and fix anything if you allow them to. The beautiful black women in my family proved this to me year after year.

My grandmother is one of the greatest heroes this earth has ever seen. Her soul is so selfless and beautiful that we are all blessed to be in her presence. She's purer than anyone I have ever met in my life. This is a woman who was born in 1926 to loving parents. She is a beautiful angel and met her king as a teenager. They went on to raise nine children who continue to carry on their legacy. It's not only because I was a grandma's boy and she did everything for me, but it's also what she did for me that I wasn't aware of at the time. She had so much love for me and everyone in my family that she protected us all even from one another. When my mom was struggling, she continued to guide us and give us opportunities that we wouldn't have had without her. When we didn't have food to eat, she cooked a full meal. When we didn't have a place to sleep, she created an atmosphere where we all could sleep peacefully. When she was down to her last dollars on her fixed income, she easily gave it to us. She and my grandfather did this for a lot, if not all their children. She is just one example of the power and strength of a black woman. This wasn't a onetime deal though. She raised her daughters to be strong women who touch everyone they meet.

My grandmother was so strong that she birthed nine children. My mom is the youngest of four daughters. Aunt Cathy, the oldest of all children, is someone that never ceases to amaze me. Though she looks to be in her mid 40's, Aunt Cathy is 72 years old, she is vibrant and the life of every party. Her short blonde hair always struck me as a symbol of power, respect, and love. My late Aunt Brenda, God rest her soul, was magnificent in very different ways. She was feisty and commanded your attention when she walked into the room. Her twin Linda, who is one of the most loving and kind people, has always treated her nephews and nieces like her own children. That takes special strength because she had so many. The most dynamic set of twins I have ever met. I miss you, Aunt Brenda. Lastly, my mom, who I spoke on earlier is the typical baby of a family and always showed us how to respect others. She raised us to have manners which are not as common as you think nowadays. There are many other black women who have touched my life for the better, and I am forever grateful. This includes my Aunt Vanessa. She showed a tremendous heart when she took her husband's lost nephew into her home to give him a better opportunity. I'm forever indebted.

This is why nothing makes my blood boil more than seeing black children and women being mistreated when they're innocent. In 2017, black people are hated and abused day after day, doing this to my women and children spurs a new anger within me. I place only a few things above the safety of these two precious groups of people. My heart fills with hate when I see them killed or disrespected by police who don't know anything about them. I have always been a peaceful person and will always advocate for the peaceful solution until it proves irresolute. I prefer not to have confrontations with people, and I don't like to see others in confrontation either. I want you to know this, the most peaceful man can only take so much beating. My people have been beaten for generations in this country, and it's not something we will accept forever. It should really make you all think of the continual disrespect you have displayed to black people in this country. Ask yourself, "Would I be able to withstand hate for this long?" This exemplifies our power to show love for other human beings, but it will come to an abrupt stop at some point. So, please leave my black women and children alone, for everyone's sake. Not only because you are poking a hive, but also because you need us as we need you. I'd really hate to see where we all would be as humanity without the amazing black women and children of the world, especially here in America.

Ideas

1. Give urban neighborhood children a chance to experience some of the luxuries in your neighborhoods. Since we can't depend on the government to provide beautiful state of the art community centers in our neighborhoods, host a night out once a month at your facilities. Use it as an opportunity to allow children to experience interacting with one another. This way, when you see the beautiful smiles on the faces of black children, you'll realize they are just as precious as yours. On the flip side, maybe our kids can attend classes that teach them how to can attain some of the same luxuries your neighborhood does. Show them that it is possible for them to reach an economic status where they can invest back into their communities so that they don't resort to stealing from innocent people in your communities. Don't keep us caged in the hood. Unlock our cages so we can see the endless possibilities of the world.

2. Black women are constantly discriminated against. Whether it is because of their race or sex, they have always been marginalized. On the same token, they are one of the most educated groups of people our country has. They have a wide view of the miscues that privileged groups make every day. They see men make mistakes that keep us from reaching our full potential. They watch you fight to stay dominant while pushing them

farther down in society. Black women are frequently the head of households in the black community. Invite them to city meetings and forums where they can offer suggestions on what can be done to improve their communities. They have a lot of answers for our issues but are always refused a voice. Don't only invite them to meetings with government decision makers but give them reasons to come. I can guarantee that if you reward black women with opportunities for their children, they will show up in droves and discuss ways to revamp their communities. Stop leaving it up to old white men who leave and go back to their suburbs anyway.

IX.

Boiling Point

"All we wanna do is take the chains off
All we wanna do is break the chains off
All we wanna do is be free
All we wanna do is be free."

-J. Cole (Be Free)

In the continued plight to liberation, black people had some of the most influential leaders this world has ever seen guiding us. Dr. Martin Luther King Jr. was an example of grace and perseverance like we've never seen. His calm demeanor and powerful words captivated the hearts of many people in this nation. He was courageous and showed passion in the most peaceful way you could imagine. He is the example we seek as children to learn how to respect everyone we meet. No matter the differences among you and others, one common thing you should share is respect. When Dr. King led, he preached nonviolence and love. He truly believed that love with the right amount of persistence could conquer anything. Even when he was exposed to deeper parts of The System, he stood firm in his beliefs and wanted nothing but the best for everyone in this country. He gets the most recognition amongst the numerous Revolutionaries black people have provided this country with. This is for good reason because he was able to transform the minds of many people who were taught hate and racism. He led us to many milestones as a culture and as a nation. Dr. King, as a prominent member of my fraternity, Alpha Phi Alpha Fraternity, Inc., stayed steadfast in his effort to eliminate the cloud of oppression that hangs over our community. The magical aspect of this is, black people are so complex and versatile. We were equally productive under the leadership of someone who wanted the same goal but took a polarizing approach from Dr. King.

Malcolm X was a leader who led with a certain level of intelligence and determination. With his interesting upbringing as a child, came different ideas and views on race relations in this country. White people, the problem was, Dr. King's willingness to peacefully speak up for minorities made you uncomfortable. Malcolm's out spoken approach that promoted resistance also made you uncomfortable. You have proven that you do not like any way we protest no matter how we do it. What Dr. King accomplished in the South, X did on the East Coast. Many black people found themselves aligned with one or the other, but a lot of times aligned with both. They were both essential for the progression of black people.

Because of the amazing black women whom I spoke of earlier that raised me, I always knew to respect everyone. Mainly because if I didn't, let's just say what my mom would do to me, may be considered going too far. I have admired the influential Dr. King as far back as I remember. He wasn't perfect in every aspect of his life, and I truly feel like that's something he knew and battled internally. This always made him more human to me, and there are many aspects of him that I'd like to incorporate into my own life. I have always been very curious as to the differences in people. Anything that is outside what I've always known and grown up around immediately sparks my interest. To me, it takes too much effort to hate or hurt someone, unless they cross the ultimate line. I'm a very chill and relaxed person. I don't necessarily seek the spotlight, but I am very vocal on how I feel, and I have no problem letting you know what my feelings are. Especially if I think it may cure you of some detrimental biases.

I genuinely feel like there are some good white people out there. I myself have come across several of them in my lifetime. You all are people just like me. You don't know what you don't know. That is part of my reason for writing this book. I know that this is how a lot of you communicate with one another when you want to keep information from my people and myself. I'm trying to bring the information to you that a lot of you refuse to seek out. Since you all are humans as well, you don't think about things that don't affect you every day. Injustices rarely affect you. There aren't too many places you go to and feel uncomfortable because everyone always looks like you. Out of sight, out of mind is a concept that we all struggle with. Now though, is the time for you to consciously seek out what the problem is, and do something about it.

If you really believe that the injustices in America need to be acknowledged and corrected, show me. All the rewards like naming streets after MLK, are wonderful and appreciated. Those examples don't come close to addressing the problem of racial inequality. I can't really ask you to open your eyes anymore. It needs to happen. Even though you only see the examples of this huge problem is when you tune in to the news. You're in your quiet cul-de-sacs, living your best life. It's bad for you because you won't realize there's a problem until it's too late. Racial injustices divide you too; it affects us all. We're all here together, so it's in your best interest to join us in this fight. You being nice to us to make yourself feel good is not enough anymore. So, if you're not in the fight with us, you're against us in my eyes until proven otherwise. That goes for all of you, the ones at work, my white friends that I currently have and the ones I have yet to meet. You may be wondering how in the world you can help. We know that feeling far too well but it's as simple as thinking outside the box. Find some black kids with a talent and give them access to your network pool. Allow them to showcase their talents to a broader audience. The audience in high places. Think about what the root issues are, and how you can affect change in your own world. We aren't the only people losing our lives over this stuff anymore. You all are losing lives too.

Besides MLK and Malcolm X, there was a young man by the name of Huey P. Newton who fought for his people on the west coast. Newton was raised here in the Bay Area, one of the most progressive areas in America. Newton was quoted explaining that he was taught to be ashamed for being black. He took the approach as a social activist after his many years of education. His goal was to provide for his communities since the government decided not to. He also had enough of police brutality and made it known that he would meet force with force. He was a young Revolutionary who deeply cared for his community. They painted him and the Black Panther Party as violent criminals, even though their only intent was to react to violence instead of sitting back and let the police pick them off one by one.

I sit here on the day after the Charlottesville, Virginia protests and riots. During a torch-bearing white supremacists rally on the campus of the University of Virginia. The protestors were met with anti-hate counter-protesters. There have reportedly been three deaths as a result of the violence. One of which is a young white woman. A white woman with a heart of courage and love. She was run over by a speeding car that targeted a group of counter-protesters. Also, I'd like to commend everyone who was out there standing up in the face of hate. Based on the footage I saw, it looked to actually be majorly white people. If my people were there, the white supremacists would have worn their police and swat uniforms alongside their torches. These brave souls who went to meet hatred in the face are the people to look to if you don't know what to do.

Another one of my closest friends, Darius speaks on this exact topic during our conversation. "I don't want you to feel down or ashamed of your privilege. You have it so now what?" Currently, Darius is a school administrator and earning his Ph.D. from Columbia University. He's like the old soul of the group and is always about his business. It took him a while to adjust to our way of constantly roasting one another. This goes for everyone though, what are you going to do now? Are you black and feel like there is a boot on your neck preventing you from reaching your full potential? Ok, what's a creative way to help the situation for you and others around you? White people, have you recently been awakened to the harm your people have caused for so many years? Use your privilege to advocate for social equality amongst your peers. I'm not saying step up to the front lines like Colin Kaepernick, but attempt to improve the life of one person. Strive to be the person that can look past their own biases and what they've always known to the point where they are fighting injustice against their own people on the other side. That's courage, but it's about time. I do believe that the last straw was the white supremacists hailing neo-nazi chants and flags. Keeping black people oppressed is one thing but threatening one's Jewish heritage is another story. No matter why you choose to fight injustice, do so with bravery and with the intent of representing all people. That was the first time I saw you all publicly stand up in solidarity against white supremacy and I was impressed.

I will forever recognize Dr. King for his accomplishments in Civil Rights. Though, it is the teachings of Malcolm X that have garnered my attention in the recent years. Newton inspires me every day with his belief in helping his community with his own hands. I'll continue to look for alternatives to violence just because that is who I am. I have not gotten to the point where I will encourage it. I will personally not sit back and watch abuse, be it physical or mental. All three of these aforementioned men strive for a better life for people who look like them. The three men garnered the attention of all people and were all assassinated by your racist uncles.

Whether they were violent or peaceful, all three of them were viewed as threats and taken out. It is the same as today when we are told that we can't protest this way or that. We know that you won't be happy with how we go about change, but that's a lot of nerve. Any way we speak out, it is going to make you uncomfortable, but I ask that you just listen, instead of trying to take our lives.

My reaction in real time to hate will be difficult for me to control. I more so demand your respect not plead for it. I want nothing to do with somehow overturning your power and keeping it for myself. All I ask for is a level playing field where we can compete and make one another better. I will not stand for anymore hate and disrespect towards my people. We've sacrificed too much and come too far to let it continue. I am just as intelligent and capable of great things just as you are. You have no right to keep rights away from me. I guarantee that this will only get worse and we will lead ourselves to some of the darkest times in our history, where no one wins, and all parties are exterminated. We are currently threatened by a nation that is known to build up its nuclear arsenal. Because of your hate for one of the best US Presidents to ever serve in the position, you chose the man who entices confrontation from all sides on his Twitter account. I have already determined that fighting for the equal rights of my brothers and sisters will be a lifelong struggle. It's starting right now. If you care about the future generations of this nation, then you stop leaving us out here fighting this massive mansion of The System by ourselves.

Afterword

A little under a decade ago, the strongest Nation in the world elected its first leader, who looked like he could be related to me. After over a century, black people finally garnered the respect we deserve. We finally saw something that older generations never thought they'd see. I was a first-time voter in 2008, and even then, I knew I was about to be a part of something special. Something special did happen, we had finally turned the corner from racism and oppression to reach the highest office in the country. This was a big deal for us all; you must understand this.

Then my fresh eyes and mind did everything but guarantee progression in America. I knew we were on our way to making a real dent in the country's old prejudices and systematic oppression which had plagued us for far too long. As a Midwesterner, cautiously, I would assume that the white people I met truly respected me with no prejudiced feelings. There was no way I would assume someone was racist without knowing anything about them. Dr. King taught us that. Two terms later, many believed America was on the path to electing its first woman, right after electing its first black man. I will forever remember the white lash that occurred by electing an openly racist, misogynistic white man with no political experience in any level of government, to the highest office in our land.

After the night of Tuesday, November 8, 2016, I was very hurt but not overly shocked. I know that's probably what everyone says, but it's the truth. I watched him beat out so many other candidates who were more qualified for the nomination. I watched his rallies with huge electric crowds become livelier, even after the leaking of his repulsive remarks regarding women. I watched him battle scandal after scandal like it held no weight during his job interview. I wouldn't get a job at McDonald's if my hiring manager heard me make such shrewd remarks. So, I knew that he was not a lock in to lose the election as the media portrayed him to be. So now what? No one seems to really have the answers. Black people have never been short of opinions, but we were all lost for words.

I purposely tried my best to leave out as much talk as I could about the 45th President of the United States. As I was writing this book, he has been elected, inaugurated and served in his role. We have endured listening to him talk about groping a woman's most private part of her body, to calling NFL protesters "sons of bitches." He has remained silent about the violence that erupted in Charlottesville following a white supremacists protest. He has spent his time as President, on the golf course, trying to send immigrants back to their countries, and engaging in Twitter wars with the likes of Steph Curry and Kim Jong Un.

Under his presidency, divisive rhetoric has become the norm and remains stationed in the media headlines. With our nation's leader making headlines every day because of his insensitive and shrewd comments, it is no wonder people with his views feel empowered to express their bigotry. It's also no wonder that as we hear about scandalous reports involving our President, to the extent that minorities have lost hope in attaining equal opportunities in life.

I will not give 45 the satisfaction of being discussed in this book that is intended for the progression of race relations in our country. The idea of hate and bigotry has no place between the pages of a project that I've developed so diligently. Does hate really benefit you in life? The group of people you hate will never be oppressed enough for you to be satisfied, so why even waste your time? You were taught to hate, and your hate will lead to your demise. If you spent some of that same energy, figuring out why exactly NFL players kneel for the anthem, you wouldn't be so offended when they do. When we riot, you don't agree with our protests, when NBA players wear warm-up shirts that say, "I can't breathe," you don't like that either. When NFL players kneel during a National Anthem, they are "sons of bitches." We shout Black Lives Matter because The System tells us time and time again that they don't. You cannot and will not silence us. The more you attempt to during our peaceful protests, the louder we will become. The louder we become, the less peaceful our protests will be. You have to understand that you can only hold your foot on our necks for so long before you are knocked down on your back.

At this point, the leaders of the current administration are not interested in representing all Americans. There are so many ties to white supremacy in the white house that they get offended when we call them out on it. I don't expect you to know how it feels to be targeted by hate groups with no government organization there to represent you. 45's lack of response to the events in Charlottesville was actually loud and clear. White supremacists took a young woman's life, and because of her views, the President could care less. He is evil and will not only ruin our lives but your lives too. He is unqualified and not fit to be President, therefore everything you trust your leader to handle, he will mishandle, and we will suffer for it.

White people, you need the support of minorities. We make up a large amount of the population, and when North Korea comes knocking, you'll be looking to us for help. Our intelligence and charisma will not be at your disposal. Our strong bodies and brave souls will not be available for battle. Believe it or not, you are not more superior to the North Koreans or us. You are not immortal, and if you continue to support the ignorance spewed from the white house, you will eventually be knocked down. White women voted for someone who is proud to grab you by the genitalia. Your hate for me led you to go with someone who has no respect for you, and I will never understand that. Your hate for me led you to put nuclear codes into the hand of a man who cannot even take constructive criticism. Your hate for me led you to elect someone who has never held any political office to the highest office in the land. I mean, he has no idea what he is doing. His combination of ignorance and bigotry is a recipe for disaster.

This is why this book is so important. Read it, critique it, and share it with friends. You are human, and you are wired to love. We were created to live together and work with one another to achieve things unimaginable. Right now, the unimaginable is social equality. That's unimaginable, but just like walking on the moon, or the crafting of bridges and skyscrapers all across the world, this too can be achieved. It only requires you to challenge the generational hatred for my people. You can be that hero who has a hand in changing the trajectory of our nation. Now is more important than ever because if we allow 45 to go on any longer, the rest of the world will handle our issues for us. Thank you all so much for choosing to give this piece a chance. It's been an honor to hold your attention. No matter what race you are, I hope you learned something or even decided to spend some time figuring out what you can do from your position to actually problem solve.

Please visit www.canibereal.com to join the conversations that are brainstorming actual solutions to the issues discussed. I hope this book inspired you to think critically and understand that even you can have a part in pulling down the walls of hatred in our country. I love you all!

Made in the USA
Columbia, SC
20 February 2018